SKETCHES IN PRISON CAMPS:

A CONTINUATION OF

Sketches of the War.

BY

CHARLES C. NOTT,

LATE COLONEL OF THE 176TH NEW YORK VOLS.

> "On her bier,
> Quiet lay the buried year;
> I sat down where I could see,
> Life without and sunshine free—
> Death within!"

SECOND EDITION.

NEW-YORK:
ANSON D. F. RANDOLPH,
770 BROADWAY, CORNER OF 9TH ST.

1865.

Entered, according to Act of Congress, in the year 1865, by

CHARLES C. NOTT,

In the Clerk's Office of the District Court of the United States for the Southern District of New York.

To

CLARKSON N. POTTER,

FOR HIS GENEROSITY AND GREAT FAITHFULNESS TO ME,

AND TO EVERY SOLDIER WITH WHOM HE HAS BEEN IN ANY WAY CONNECTED

DURING THE PAST WAR,

THIS WORK IS GRATEFULLY DEDICATED.

CONTENTS.

PRISON CAMPS.

I.

THE TRANSPORT.

"THERE come the tug-boats, Colonel," says an officer, as I stand on the deck of the "Alice Counce," waiting for my regiment. I am a stranger to it, and only assume command to-day. From the East river come the boats, laden as many other boats have been, with a dark swarm of men, who cover the deck and hang upon the bulwarks.

The boats come alongside and throw their lines to the ship, and then rises a concord of those sounds that generally start with a new regiment.

"ATTENTION! Officers and men will remain on board the boats till ordered aboard the ship. Captains of A and F will march their companies aboard and conduct them to their quarters. The bunks of each are marked with their Company letter."

The hubbub ends, and the companies climb successively aboard, and stumble down into the dark hold, where, cold and clammy from recent scrubbings, are certain rough bunks, each so contrived as thoroughly to make four men unhappy. Unhappy! for the bunks are three tiers thick between decks, leaving no room wherein to sit up and be sick—and four men in one bed never did and never will lie still. Those who have never been to sea before, dream not of what awaits them!

Yet the men surprise me with the great good humor in which they seek out and take possession of their dark quarters. On one side, beginning at the sternmost bulkhead, Co. "A," with the aid of dingy ship-lanterns, stows away the baggage, and next to it is "F," at the same work. This order of the companies has a reason; for in line of battle, they are assorted in pairs, called "divisions," so that each division shall contain one of the five senior and one of the five junior captains. In camp too they occupy the same places as in line of battle, and hence this is the proper guide for assigning quarters on ship board. Beginning on one side at the extreme stern with "A," we run round the ship until at the extreme stern on the opposite side we finish with "B." There is some difference in the comfort of the bunks; somebody must have the worst, and it is very desirable that this somebody shall blame for it only his own bad luck.

"Shall we weigh anchor soon, Captain?"

"Can't tell, sir. No wind now. Looks as though a fog were coming down. Can't sail till we've a wind."

"Colonel," says one of the Captains, "my first-lieutenant has not been out of camp for six weeks. If you will let him go ashore, I shall be much obliged."

"I cannot, Captain; the ship is ordered to sail immediately. While this is possible, no officer can leave."

"Colonel," says another, "Lieutenant A., of my company, learnt last evening that his mother is quite ill. Will you approve this pass?"

"I am sorry to say, Captain, that no officer can leave the ship. We are under sailing orders—the pilot is on board—the tug within hail, and we shall weigh anchor whenever the wind freshens."

"It is really very hard."

"Very!"

"Colonel," says a third, "my first-sergeant's wife is very ill. I told him that he could go back and see her, and get his things this morning. If you will approve this pass, I shall be very much obliged."

"He must send for his things. We are under sailing orders. No one can leave the ship."

"The poor fellow promised her that he would certainly be back to-day. It was the only way he could make her consent to his coming. He is a most faithful fellow."

"Mate, do you think we can possibly sail to-night?"

"No, sir; fog won't rise afore midnight. Pilot's gone ashore."

"Then, Captain, let your sergeant take this dispatch to headquarters, and report on board at daylight."

The fog grows denser and denser—the rain comes down; such dreary refusals and disappointments have filled the day. The cabin will not hold half the officers. Nothing is settled—all is dirt, disorder and confusion. Oh, what a wretched, moody, miserable day!

A week of such days passes, but at last the fresh west wind blows keen and cold. A little tug comes out from among the piers, and seizing the great vessel, leads her towards the Narrows, and the regiment at last is moving to New Orleans.

"I shall be glad," says a young lieutenant, flushed with the thought of setting forth on his first campaign, "I shall be glad when we are out of sight of New York."

"You'll be gladder when you come in sight of it again."

"Perhaps I shall," he says, with a laugh; "but after all our working and waiting, it's delightful to be off at last."

I stand on the deck watching the sinking city and the lessening shores, as many have done before me, while gliding down the beautiful bay, until they grow dim in the distance, and then turn away, to think of inspections, rations, fires, and sea-sickness.

The first night has passed without incident or accident, extinguishing the excitement of our sailing and leaving us to wake up quietly for our first day at sea. Not "quietly," for twenty drummer boys, without the faintest sign of sea-sickness, rattled out a reveille that frightened the rats from their holes, and brought the sleeping watch from the forecastle, and disturbed every sailor and sleeper in the ship. It left us wide awake, and ready for the routine and duties of the day.

BREAKFAST!—Breakfast is no easy thing to get in a transport ship. All night long two gangs of cooks have been at work, and there are fears and whispers that with all their efforts, the breakfast will run short. Very aggravating is it to wait for breakfast in this cold sea air, with nothing else to think of, and your thoughts quickened (if you are among the last) by the fear that there is not enough to go round. A serious business, too, it is to deal it out, requiring more than an hour of hungry moments. The companies form in files, and on each side of the ship approach the caboose. A mug and plate are thrust through a hole. In a moment, filled with a junk of pork, three "hard-tack," and a pint of pale coffee, they are thrust back. The hungry owner seizes them and hurries away to some quiet spot, where he can unclasp his knife and fork, and cool his coffee to his liking. The long files of the unfed, one by one, creep slowly up to the greasy dispensary. The first company of the occasion ironically congratulates the last, the last ironically condoles with the first. They take turn about. Company A is first at breakfast to-day; second at lunch; third at supper: to-morrow it will be fourth; and thus it will keep on until at length it reaches the agonizing state of being *last!*

WATER!—The water is the next annoyance of the

morning. The men are brought up on the upper deck. On the lower one is a pump connected by a hose, with the water casks below. The mate, on behalf of the ship, and an officer, on behalf of the regiment, deal out the water. Two men from every squad, each with a load of canteens hung around his neck, come forward and fill them from the tub—a slow and mussy piece of work.

INSPECTION.—"The water is dealt out, Colonel," says the Officer of the Day. "Will you inspect the quarters?"

The assembly beats, and the men again crowd the upper deck. Armed with a lantern, I grasp a slippery ladder, and go down into the dark, "between decks." It is very still and almost empty there, much like a gloomy cave. The companies have been divided into four squads, and a sergeant and two corporals have charge of the quarters of each.

I begin with the first and poke the lantern up into the upper tier, over into the middle tier, down into the lower tier. Blankets out—knapsacks at the head—nothing lying loose. No crumbs betraying hard-tack smuggled in; the deck scrubbed clean. "Very good, Sergeant. Your quarters do you credit." The next, a blanket not out—half a hard-tack in the upper tier, the crumbs scattered over the lower—the deck dingy with loathsome tobacco. "Look at this, and this, and this, Sergeant. Yours are the only dirty quarters in the ship."

"Don't you think the quarters pretty good on the whole, Colonel?" asks the Officer of the Day.

Very good, Captain. If we except that sergeant's, there is really nothing to find fault with." And thus ends the first inspection.

"If the rebels hadn't ha' destroyed the light-house," remarks my friend the first mate, as he looks with his glass toward Hampton Roads, "we could ha' run right straight in last night, but seeing that the ship is light in ballast, and a good many souls aboard, why, it wasn't safe."

"So they destroyed the Cape Henry light, did they?"

"Yes indeed, they did, and it does seem to me that of all they've done that ought to ha' set the hull civilized world against them, it's the worst. Just think now how many a fine vessel must ha' gone aground there, and never be got off again, just for want of the light; why, it does seem to me that it's worse than a shooting women and children; at any rate, it's just the same."

"There comes the pilot-boat, and she has her signal set," says some one.

Far up the Chesapeake the pilot-boat is seen, a small flag fluttering from her mast head. She comes straight as an arrow, like a greyhound rushing down upon us in his play. How beautifully she bounds along, looking as she mounts the waves as if she would leap from the water. The yards are backed and the ship stops and waits for the little craft. The pilot-boat circles round her, and coming into the wind, seems to settle down like a dog resting from his sport. A little cockle shell of a boat puts off, pulled by two black oarsmen, who buffet and dodge the waves, and make their way slowly against the wind toward the ship. There is much curiosity to see this Virginian pilot, and all hands crowd forward as he comes up the side. The Captain alone has not moved to meet him. *He* stands dignifiedly on the poop deck, his glass beneath his arm. The pilot does not ask for him, or pause or look around; he evidently knows the very spot on which the Captain stands. He bows to the crowd around him, pushes his way through, and mounts to the deck. He walks up to the Captain, and they shake hands. The Captain hands him his glass: the pilot takes it: it is the emblem of authority, and the Captain no longer commands the ship.

The pilot raises the glass and looks sharply in one direction; he takes a turn or two up and down the deck, and looks attentively in another. I am convinced that he knows as well where we are as I should, were I standing on the steps of the City Hall. All this looking is evidently done to impress beholders with the difficulty of being a pilot. "How does she head?" says the pilot. "Due west," says the man at the wheel. "Keep her west by sou' half sou'," says the pilot. "Wes' by sou' half sou'," responds the man at the wheel. "Set your jib, sir," says the pilot to the Capt. "Set the jib, Mr. Small," says the Captain to the first mate. "Set the jib, Mr. Green," says the first mate to the second mate. "All hands man the jib halyards," says the second mate. "Aye, aye, sir," respond the sailors, and the soldiers look quite sober at finding themselves all of a sudden in so difficult and maybe dangerous a channel. Meanwhile the black oarsmen pull back to where the pilot-boat still lies at rest. The touch of the cockle shell upon her side startles her again into life. She shakes her white wings, and turning, bounds off toward another ship, whose sails are slowly rising from the waves far off toward the east.

What we have come to Fortress Monroe for no one can tell. In spite of a decisive order to sail forthwith for New Orleans, the wind refuses to blow. Another weary week of calm and fog intervenes. The Captain laments and growls, and says if we had kept on with *that* breeze, we could have been at the Hole-in-the-wall, and maybe at Abacom-light; but now there's no telling when the wind will set in from the west—he's known it set this way at this season for three weeks. The officers and men repeat the growls and lamentations, and fail not to ask me five hundred times a day what we have come to Fortress Monroe for.

The week of waiting ends, and a westerly wind assures us that we may start. "We must have a tug to tow us down," says the Captain. "And we must have the water-boat along side," says the mate. A boat load of officers and soldiers go ashore to make their last purchases. I wait on the dock and watch the water-boat as it puts off, and listen to the "yo he yo" on the "Alice

Counce" and "Emily Sturges," which tells me that their anchors are coming up.

The tug took us down—the pilot left us much as before, and we are now out at sea. The "Emily" led us by half an hour, and all day long was in sight, sailing closer to the wind and standing closer on the coast. As the evening closed in, we cast many jealous glances toward her, and asked each other which ship would be ahead in the morning.

The second day was a gloomy, wintry day, with a rising wind, and constantly increasing sea; and the second night out I felt the motion grow and grow, but thought it rather pleasant, and had no fears of evil consequences. I rose with the reveille, which seemed fainter than usual, steadied myself out of the cabin, and still knew no fear. I reached the deck and found that but four drummer boys rub-a-dubbed, and but few men had come up from below. I mounted to the poop deck, and there I found three lieutenants. There was something unusual about them. Two sat very still braced against a spar, while the third staggered violently up and down with a pale, in fact a ghastly face, and kept saying in a jolly manner to himself, "How are *you*, ship? how are *you*, o–oh–shun?"

"This is very strange," thought I. "But perhaps they're ill. I'll ask them."

"Gentlemen, are you sick—sea-sick?"

"Sick? oh no!"

Nobody was sick, so I turned and looked down on the

main deck. The reveille had ended, yet the number on deck had not increased. A sergeant with five or six men in line was calling his roll in a loud voice, at which he and half his men repeatedly laughed, as though absence from roll-call was a capital joke.

It is usual for an officer from each company to come up to me immediately after the morning roll-call, and report the state of his company, "all present or accounted for," or so many present and so many absent and not accounted for. I am somewhat strict about it, yet on this morning only one or two reported. I thought this negligence strange—unaccountable—yet for some reason or other, I did not go down and ascertain the cause of it. I turned toward the east. The sun was near his rising, and the crimson light filled the sky and tinged the white foam of the tossing waves. It was a splendid sight, and brought to mind one of the finest sea pieces of the Dusseldorf. I stood watching the wide expanse of heaving billows—the cloud-spotted sky under-lit with rays of the coming sun—the unnumbered waves breaking in long rolls of foam, silvered and gilded by the glowing east. I was lost in admiration, when I suddenly felt—sick! I made brave attempts to keep myself up—to weather it out—to stay on my legs—to stay on deck—to do something—to do anything. In vain!

That day the wind increased and blew a gale. Through the long hours of the afternoon the vessel plunged and tossed. Furniture broke loose and slid backward and forward across the cabin. The steward looked in, seized the vagrant pieces, and lashed them fast. Stragglers steadied themselves from door to table and from table to sofa, to say that all the others were down—that they began to feel a little qualmish, and that affairs were growing serious. Toward midnight there was a tremendous shock—the ship staggered and stood still, as though she had struck upon a rock; in an instant more the door of the forward cabin was burst open with a crash, and in another the water broke through the sky-light over my head, and poured, a torrent, on the cabin floor. To the men between decks it seemed a shipwreck. Yet there were not wanting a few heartless wretches, who, neither sea-sick nor frightened, made sport of all the others. "The ship's struck a breaker," roared one of these from his bunk. "All frightened men roll out and put on their boots to sink in." "Struck," "breakers," "sinking," sounded around, and several hundred men rolled out in the darkness, and frantically tried to put on their boots. With the next roll, away all hands went. Some caught at the bunks—some clutched each other—the penitent prayed—the wicked swore—the frightened blubbered—the sick and philosophical lay still. In the midst of the sliding, the scramble and the din, a voice rose from another bunk, "Captains"—it thundered in the style of a Colonel on drill—"rectify the alignment." And the jokers added to the din their loud laughs of derision.

A little later the mate came in—a large, stalwart

sailor, seeming a giant in his oilskins and sou'wester. He carefully closed the door, stepped lightly across the cabin floor, ceremoniously removed his hat, and looking into the darkness of the captain's state-room, said in the most apologetic of tones, "Captain Singer, I'm really afraid the mast will go, if we don't ease her a point. It works very bad, and the wind's rising."

The Captain considered slowly and said, "Ease her."

The mate said politely, "Yes, sir," and then backed across the cabin lightly on tip toe, hat in hand, opened the door slowly and noiselessly, and then, without replacing his hat, slipped out into the storm.

The long night wore away and was followed by a longer day. The ship tossed and plunged, rising as though she were mounting from the water to the sky, and then sinking as though she would never stop. At last the gale blew itself out, and then came a calm, when the ship lay like a log on the water, rolling ceaselessly from side to side, and creaked and groaned with every toss and roll. But now there is a cry of land, and the sick drag themselves to the deck and look toward a rocky island of the Bahama group, which is the "land." How beautiful it seems, hung there on the horizon between the shifting clouds and tossing sea! The breeze is fair, the sea not rough, and we soon draw nearer to this land. On the farther end rises the snowy tower of the light-house, and beside it stands the house of the keeper. No other house, nor field, nor tree, nor blade of grass adorns this huge bare rock. The waves have worn grooves on the steep sides, and up these the water dashes, and runs down in white moving columns. Abreast of us is a strange opening in the wall-like rock, which has given to the island its name of "Hole-in-the-wall." The spy-glasses disclose a man, a woman, and some children, looking toward the ship. Once in three months the supply ship will visit them, bringing their food, their clothing, their water and the oil: once or twice a year, when the sea is calm and the wind has fallen, the keeper may row out to some ship to beg for newspapers; more often they may gaze, as they are gazing now, at passing vessels; and thus, with such rare intervals, they pass their lonely life, cut off and isolated from all mankind.

The warm temperature and rich blue color of the water tell us that we are in the Gulf Stream. As I lie upon the deck looking upon the mysterious current, a slender bird, eight or ten inches long, shining like silver, flits through the air. "Did you see that bird?" asks more than one voice. "Was it a bird?" "Yes, it flew like one." "No, it came out of the water and went back there."

"It's a flying-fish, gentlemen," says the mate; "you'll see plenty of them soon."

A more beautiful, fairy-like sight than these flying-fish present, I have seldom seen. A delicate creature, bright and silvery, and often beautifully tinged with blue, emerges from the water, and soars just above the waves in a long, graceful, bird-like flight, until striking against the summit of some wave that lifts its white cap higher than the rest, it disappears.

This is called a pleasant voyage from Hole-in-the-wall. We watch the flying-fish, catch Portuguese men-of-war, and bathe in the warm water of the stream, until there appears before us what some at first thought a mud bank, but which now proves to be another ocean of muddy water.

"It is the Mississippi," says the Captain. "The river must be up, for we're a hundred miles good from the Sou'west Pass. There'll be trouble in crossing the bar; when the river's up the water's down."

As we draw nearer, the contrast between the two oceans grows more plain. The line is as distinct as that between land and water on a map. Now the bow of the vessel reaches it—now the line is a midship—now I look down upon it, and now the ship floats wholly in the water of the Mississippi.

The muddy sea has raised a ferment of excitement, and many, who have all faith in the ship's reckoning, still look forward as though they could look through the hundred miles before us, and see the wished-for land. Night closes, however, leaving us surrounded by the same muddy waves; but we turn in, with the strong assurance that to-morrow we shall make the Pass.

Land! But hidden under low fogs, that, I am told, brood over this delta of the Mississippi. From the cross-trees can be seen one or two steam-tugs, vessels at anchor, and distant salt marshes; but from the deck we peer about in all directions, and see nothing in the fog. A pilot moves the ship up to her anchorage. We are to wait perhaps only the moving of the tugs—perhaps the falling of the river; the river is up, and as was foretold by the Captain, the water is down.

The explanation of this paradox is simple. The water on the bar is ocean water, though discolored by the river. Its height is always a tidal height, that is, it rises with the tide, not with the river. The freshets, while they do not add to the height of the water, nevertheless bring down large quantities of mud, which settles on the bar, and thus builds up the bottom without raising the surface of the water. The pilots measure from the bottom, and finding it nearer the surface than it was, say that the water has fallen, when in fact it is the bottom that has risen. Then come the tides and wash away the loose mud upon the bar, and thus the water deepens while the river falls.

We are again at anchor; a tug is heard in the fog, and all turn anxiously toward it. The Captain of the tug hails the Captain of the ship, and demands what water she draws.

"Sixteen feet and a half," is the answer. "Will that do?"

The Captain of the tug says it is doubtful—they are going down to tug another ship that draws fifteen and a half, and if they get her over, they will tug us at the next flood tide.

That ship is the transport "William Woodbury." She

comes down gallantly, the soldiers crowding her bulwarks, two powerful tugs puffing at her sides, and every sail set. We watch her with anxiety. She passes a buoy that we think marks the bar, and all seems well. The mate says he "don't know but akind of believes she's over." As he speaks, she swings round, stops, and sticks fast. The steam-tugs pull her backward and forward and sidewise, and at last over the bar; she disappears in the fog beyond, and we await with fresh anxiety the flood-tide of the afternoon.

These tugs have one strange appendage in the form of a ladder as high as the smoke-pipe; on the top of this is a chair, and in this chair is a man. It is the pilot who thus looks over the low fogs of the Pass. From this high place we hear the voice of one, toward evening, and soon two tugs come down to try their strength in dragging our ship through two feet of mud. The heaviest hawser is out on deck and an end run over either side to the stubborn little tug that lies there. The anchor is tripped, a sail or two set, and with good headway, we approach the bar. Suddenly every one who is on his legs takes an unexpected step forward—the hawser parts—the tugs break loose—and we are hard aground. But the tugs do not give it up. They reattach themselves and drag us, after many efforts, out of the mud and back to where we started.

We approach the bar again cautiously; but again we feel the vessel grounding, and again she stands still. The tugs tug away as though striving to drag us through by main strength, and many declare that we are moving slowly. A neighboring buoy, however, stays close beside us, and after half an hour's hard work, shows that we have not moved a foot. Still the tugs tug as obstinately as ever. They drag us back and try afresh—now to the right—now to the left—panting, puffing and blowing. The pilots sit enveloped in clouds of black coal smoke, and shout, and scream. At last, with the last rays of daylight, and the last swelling of the tide, and the last strands of the hawser, and at the moment when all efforts must cease, we are dragged across the bar, and enter the Mississippi.

II.

THE PAY-MASTER.

WESTWARD from New Orleans stretches the Opelousas railroad, and along this road we are now doing guard duty. Guarding a railroad is the most unwelcome task that can be thrust on the Colonel of a new regiment—scattering the companies, demoralizing the men, destroying the regiment, and therefore a Colonel, under such circumstances, has a right to be a little discontented, and very cross.

I *am* a little discontented, and have wished a hundred times that I were back, writing on the sunny hill-side of Camp Lowe, enduring all the hardships of Tennessee. From an unsoldierly point of view, there is nothing to complain of here. For the leaky tent, the muddy floor, the pork and "hard-tack" of the West, my large new tent has a double-fly and plank floor; and it is filled with tables, chairs, and other luxuries. Up the neighboring bayou of La Fourche, too, come miniature canal-boats, tugged along by little creole ponies, and laden with fish and oysters, which the swarthy French fishermen catch in the not distant Gulf. The surrounding woods are filled with game that finds its way constantly to camp, and from every one of the large plantations that abound here, are brought vegetables, eggs and poultry. Yet I do not relish this ease and indolence—the rough cavalry service suits me better, and I wish a hundred times a day that I were back in Tennessee.

It is the spring-time of the year, yet there is but little of the reality of spring to us. The grass has long been green, the flowers are plentiful, the sun is hot and burning, but the leaves come leisurely along, and for a fortnight have only moved. These flowers, too, have generally no fragrance, though now and then there is one that overpowers us with its sweet, sickening odor, and the birds that fill the trees are songless, save the "merry mocking-bird," who, like the perfume giving flowers, has more than his share of noise and song. There is, therefore, none of the glad bursting forth that makes so brief and beautiful our northern spring.

This is a muster-day in the army, and it is the forerunner of the Pay-Master. I have been busy since daybreak calling the rolls of the companies along the railroad, and I have now to ride twelve miles and muster one that is doing Provost guard duty in the village of Houma. It is not a pleasant ride to Houma; the road runs along a bayou, as straight and stagnant as a canal. Occasionally there comes a boat, freighted with a dozen barrels of molasses or a few hogsheads of sugar, furrowing its way through the green scum that covers the water, and breaking down the rank-growing weeds that choke the channel. The vagabond-looking ponies that drag it along, travel on the "levee," which has the appearance of a tow-path, and makes the bayou look more than ever like a canal. This bayou is a hideous frog-pond, long drawn out, filled with black, slimy mud, and teeming with hideous reptiles. My horse starts as I ride beside it, and snuffs the tainted air nervously, for two turkey-buzzards fly up from the huge carcass of an alligator, and alight close beside me on the fence. Two more remain on the alligator, gorged so that they cannot rise. Their rough, dirty feathers remind one of the uncombed locks of a city scavenger. No one ever shoots them, but draws back and says, with unconcealed disgust, "What a foul bird that is."

Yet on the other side of the road, spreading back to the poisonous swamps in the rear, lie some of the rich plantations of Louisiana. There are the sugar-houses, with their heavy brick chimneys, as large and clumsy as those of a foundry; and near by stand the planter's house, the overseer's house, the engineer's house, and a little village of contraband cabins. The vast fields are cut up into square blocks by ditches, sometimes ten feet deep, reminding one of the graded lots in the outskirts of a city. On one side of each range of these blocks is a raised plantation road, which crosses the ditches on substantial bridges, and runs, perhaps for miles, arrow-like, as a railroad. It is probable that the plantation is surrounded by a levee, to keep the water out. The large ditches then empty into a canal, and at the end of this canal will be found a "pumping machine," driven by a steam engine, which pumps the plantation dry and keeps it above water. Such wealthful agriculture we have nowhere in the North.

The broad, dull thoroughfare on which I ride is an unpleasant contrast to the shaded bridle-roads of Tennessee. Yet it furnishes our only ride, and for twelve miles there is but one turn-off, or intersecting road, and not one hill or hollow. So far as the eye can reach in all directions—so far as one can ride on any road he may choose to take, is one weary, continuing, unbroken flatness. I feel a constant longing to mount a hill, and often have to repress an impulse to climb a tree, where I can look around and breathe a little freer air.

Houma looks somewhat like a deserted village. The shops are shut, many of the houses empty, and the scowling people wear an idle, listless air. There is no love lost between them and the troops. Some months ago a few sick soldiers of the twenty-first Indiana were massacred not far from the village, and it was done by some of the most "respectable" planters. I believe all of the guilty parties escaped to the enemy's lines, except one, and he, poor wretch, lived for months in the gloomy swamps near us, a frightened maniac. His body was lately found, showing that he had lain down, worn out and sick, and died alone in the dreary solitude.

In one of these deserted houses I find my officers established, and after finishing the muster of their company, I spend with them a pleasant evening and quiet night. Another dull and solitary ride carries me back to my headquarters, to await the wished-for coming of the Pay-Master. A regiment which has never been paid looks eagerly for that admired and much respected functionary. It understands not why there should be delays, and coins a rumor at least once a day, that he is on his way to camp. After many disappointments, one of these rumors assumes a substantial shape. A special train comes rushing up the railroad, consisting of an engine and a single car. The train shrieks that it will stop and does so: it bears only two passengers, and a heavy, mysterious, iron-bound box. They are the Pay-Master, his clerk, and his money chest.

The Pay-Master is smiling, and happy as a man who travels with a trunk full of smiles should be. He walks through the excited throng to my tent, and the mysterious box is borne by two soldiers in a reverent manner behind him. He takes it from them at the tent in a careless sort of way, and pulls and tumbles it about as if it were a common piece of vulgar wood—he does not even glance at it as he twists and turns the mysterious lock. From its depths he brings out our pay-rolls, and says in a complimentary manner that they are correct—that indeed he never paid a new regiment where they were more correct. He shakes his head despondingly, and adds that there are some regiments in this department that have never been paid—that have never got their rolls right, and he fears never will. Our men are immensely relieved as these facts are whispered around, and acquire fresh confidence in their officers,—perhaps rather more than they ever had before.

The rolls are sent back to the different companies, and the men assemble round each Captain's tent and sign them. The Pay-Master fortifies himself against the coming excitement with a little luncheon. Meanwhile a table has been placed at the opening of a tent, within which are the mysterious box and clerk.

"Now, Colonel," says the Pay-Master, "if you will be so good as to give the necessary orders, we will begin."

The Pay-Master takes his place behind the table which bars the entrance to the tent and box; the first company falls in "by one rank," faces "without doubling," and in single file approaches the Pay-Master. The Pay-Master takes a pay-roll and calls a name; the clerk takes its "duplicate" and checks the name; the owner steps forward and answers to the name. The Pay-Master seizes a bundle of the precious paper and tears off the wrapper. The notes dance through his flying fingers, and flutter down before the owner of the first name. The Pay-Master carelessly seizes them, says "sixty-three dollars, forty-five cents," and tosses them toward the owner, as though he wishes to be rid of the vulgar trash. The owner, much discomposed, carefully picks them up and hurriedly retires to the nearest bench, whereon he seats himself, and slowly counts and recounts the notes, at least five times. It is labor in vain; he cannot make them a dollar more, or a dime less than did the Pay-Master. Those practised hands, though they count the money only once, and move with the swiftness of a magician's wand, never make mistakes.

There is another day's work before the Pay-Master, and a somewhat unusual one for him. Four companies remain to be paid, and the special train has gone back to New Orleans. We must travel, therefore, by a hand-car. The mysterious box is carried to the car, the clerk sits on it, keeping a bright look-out toward the rear, lest any pursuing locomotive should rush upon us ere we know it; the Pay-Master and I seat ourselves in front upon the floor, and half a dozen soldiers, who are both guard and engine, stow themselves away as best they can, and then seizing the crank, put our little vehicle slowly in motion.

It is very pleasant skimming along swiftly so close to the ground, with so little noise or jarring, with such an absence of smoke and dust, and with such a free, unrestrained view of everything around us. By far the pleasantest ride upon the rail that any of us have ever had, is this. We fly quickly across the wide plantation that adjoins the camp, and then enter the wood or swamp, whichever you prefer to call it.

"There will be no train coming along I hope," said the Pay-Master, as he glanced at the narrow roadway and black, slimy water that came close to us on either side. "What should we do *now*, for instance?"

"Tumble the hand-car into the swamp, and slide ourselves down the sides of the road, and lie quiet till the train has passed."

"Ugh!" said the Pay-Master. "I do not like the idea of sliding myself into that water. Look how black and slimy it is, and then that unhealthy green scum upon it. I should not wonder if it were full of snakes and alligators."

"Alligators! You may say that; look there!"

An immense alligator is seen stretched on a fallen tree, and dozing in the warmth of the April sun.

"May I give him a shot?" asks the sergeant of our guard, drawing his revolver.

"Yes, if you can hit him."

The sergeant slowly raises his pistol—the hand-car stops—bang! and the bullet strikes against the scaly side and glances off. The alligator slides from the log, and disappears in the inky water.

"I don't care about making that gentleman's acquaintance," says the Pay-Master. "Mr. Clerk, please keep a sharp look-out behind for any stray locomotive that may be coming along, and the Colonel and I will look out ahead. Seven miles you say it is to the next station? Well, I shall feel a little easier when we get there."

The hand-car resumes its former speed, and we fly along through the deep shades and deeper stillness of the swamp. The rumbling of the car that we hardly heard in the open fields now echoes distinctly, and our voices almost startle us, they sound so very clear and loud. There are no fields or openings on either side, no firm ground to stand upon, and the trees rise out of the green-coated water.

"Stop! what's that? There's something ahead," calls the Pay-Master; "is it an engine?"

"No, sir," replies the sergeant, "it is the picket at Moccason Bayou."

A mile or two ahead can be dimly seen something moving where the railroad track is lost among the overhanging trees. Then, as the car lessens the distance, can be distinguished the figures of three or four men, the gleam of their muskets and the blue uniform of the United States. The picket has turned out and is watching us. Our engineer puts on a full head of steam, and our little special train rushes along faster than ever, until it is "braked-down" on the very bank of Moccason Bayou.

"These are your men, are they?" asks the Pay-Master.

"Yes, they are here guarding the bridge."

"Then I will take an order from them authorizing me to pay the money to their Captain."

The Pay-Master writes the order, and looks around with curiosity at the picket station. We peer into the bayou, which is supposed to swarm with deadly moccason snakes, and then climbing on the car, resume our jaunt. We pay the two companies stationed at Tigerville; we hearken to the commanding officer's advice to stay and dine with him, and then, with a new hand-car and a fresh guard, we run twelve miles further up the road and pay the last company. An hour or two after dark this is accomplished, and we prepare to return.

As we approach the car, one of the men meets us with a rumor that a division of the army is coming up the single track, and that doubtless we shall meet several trains where the swamp is darkest and the roadway narrowest. We investigate the rumor, and find that it is based on the fact that the trains *ought* to come, but no one really knows that they are coming. "What do you think, Pay-Master? You and the money-chest must be taken great care of." The Pay-Master thinks that if we had a lantern it would be safe. We procure a lantern, and hold a consultation. One of our guard is an experienced railroad builder; he knows the ways of hand-cars, and can tell afar off the sound of advancing trains. He promises to "brake-down" the hand-car in an instant, and to forewarn us of impending engines long before they can run into us.

We start, and the experienced man stands with his hand upon the brake, and an officer who has joined us takes his place in front, holding the lantern plainly in sight. Away we go into the darkness of the swamp—a darkness so thick that you cannot see the man who sits beside you. For several miles the road runs straight as an arrow, and I sit behind with the Pay-Master, trusting those in front to keep a look-out. At length we come out of the swamp and enter an open plantation country, through which the road makes many turns. "Ease off and then brake-down," and the car lessens its speed and in a few moments stops. The experienced man goes forward, puts one ear close to the track, and announces that there is no train on the road within ten miles. We start again, and this time I stand up and post myself where I can have a clear view of the front.

"Oh, Colonel, sit down," says the experienced man; "no use in your standing up. I'll tell you the moment any train comes in sight."

"I'm much obliged to you, but as the way is somewhat crooked from here to Tigerville, I think I shall be quite as comfortable keeping a little look-out of my own, as sitting down and trusting it all to you."

The hand-car runs merrily forward; the men, refreshed with our brief halt, are sending it along with increased speed, when through the trees and bushes, across a sharp curve of the road—a flash—a light, and the thunder of a coming train. "An engine." "The cars." "'Brake-down' quick." "They're at full speed." "They'll be on us if you don't hurry." The experienced man tugs at the brake, the others start up and frantically endeavor to extricate their legs and arms (which everybody else seems to be sitting upon), the hand-car runs on as if it will never stop; the heavy engine glares on us with its great, glowing eye, and comes rushing forward in unabated haste. There is no time to waste in trifles; the officer in front springs from the car and runs down the road, waving the lantern with all his might; a couple of soldiers tumble themselves off, and one adroitly falls across the track, and lies there stunned; the experienced man strains away on his brake; the Pay-Master and I drop off behind, and seizing hold of the car, succeed in stopping it. The train seems but a few yards distant, crashing and thundering, and shaking the very ground we stand on. The Pay-Master, who has been the most cautious of the party, is now the most cool and decided. While two men push against each other and the experienced man gives contradictory directions, the Pay-Master seizes the car, capsizes it off the track, and hurls it down the bank. The precious box and the stunned soldier are dragged out of the way, and the train goes roaring past. When all is over, we first berate the experienced man roundly, then haul the car with much trouble up the bank and on to the track, and then feel our way cautiously down to Tigerville. There we refresh ourselves with a cold supper, tell over the tale of our escape, and abuse the engineer to our heart's content for not seeing our lantern, and stopping his train. The Pay-Master announces his intention of writing the history of the last twenty-four hours, and publishing it as the "Adventures of a Pay-Master." I am sorry to say he does not keep this promise.

III.

THE WILD TEXANS.

Some weeks after the pay-day, I found myself stretched upon a bed, in a little shanty, at Tigerville. I had some hazy recollections of having moved my quarters to Tigerville—of having left my tent one evening, after dress-parade, for a ride—of having ridden to the hospital and dismounted, with a dizzy head and aching frame—of the surgeon telling me, that I was very ill and must not go back—and then of horrible fever-visions.

The long days travelled slowly, and the sultry nights wore away wearily, but they rolled into weeks ere anything was gained. Then I was carried to Brashear, and placed in a house which had been the mansion of an old Louisiana family. In front was a strip of lawn shaded by large oaks moss-hung and spreading. Beneath them the view opened on the waters of the Atchafalaya, which here had widened into Berwick Bay, and beyond, on the little village of Berwick. Around were the remains of the finest garden of western Louisiana. There still lingered thickets of the fig and orange, of lemon and banana; and there still flowered oleanders, and catalpas, and jasmin, with many other specimens of tropical fruits and flowers. As I sat observing these remnants of other times, an old New York friend and his wife came in. The lady looked around on the grass-grown walks, broken and effaced; on the long rows of fruit trees to which horses were picketed; on the rare flower-beds trampled out by droves of mules; on the smooth grass-plots covered with heaps of rubbish.

"You have been here before," I said, as I marked the careful looks that travelled so closely over every part of the sad, disordered scene.

"I have passed the most of my life here," she replied. "This is my mother's house."

It was the story of another divided family. All of her own relations were in the Confederate lines, and she had remained with her husband to await the coming of the Union army.

The enemy were gathering above us on the Teche. Those oath-taking patriots, whose sons were in the enemy's army and crops within our lines; who, heretofore, had stood aloof and scowled sullenly at us when we passed, now came into camp, and for once were communicative. They asked us if we knew what was coming, and hinted at Southern conscription, and the damage the Wild Texans would do the growing crop. They feared the rough riders from the prairies, and told many tales of their lawless cruelty. There came in, too, refugees and contrabands, all speaking of the enemy's increasing strength; of boats collecting for some night attack, and of the reckless fierceness of those Wild Texans. On the opposite side of the river, the Wild Texans began to move in open day. They came down in little scouting parties, hiding behind houses and bushes, but constantly on the alert. We must have presented tempting marks for a long-range Enfield, yet they never fired, but flitted silently about, always observing us, yet never responding to our many shots.

I watched these indications of the gathering storm, with the nervous irritability inseparable from convalescence. But every slight exertion brought on a slight relapse, and I was soon forced, so far as I could do so, to abstract myself from these excitements, and try to gather back my strength in time to be of service in the coming trouble. To this end, I took up the contents of some captured mails. There were a few of the ridiculous letters, that once found their way freely into our newspapers, with bad spelling, and false syntax, and bombastic rhetoric, but the most of them were sad. More woeful letters were never read than these Wild Texans wrote. There were such mournful yearnings for home —for peace—for those they had left behind, that, insensibly, the mind changed from exultation into pity. There was a slight compunction, too, in running the eye over the secrets of our enemies; a more than reluctance to look upon these hidden words, which love and duty had written for loving eyes, and coldly appropriate them as our own. There were tales of want and tales of love —tidings of weddings and of deaths. Here was a letter from a father in Port Hudson, to his "dear little daughters;" and here one from a mother to her "own beloved son." This is a family letter, written by the parents and sisters, to their "two dear boys," who now are watching us from the other shore. And this one is the reverse, for it is addressed to "father, mother, wife, and sisters." The rebel soldier has filled his "last sheet" with sad forebodings, with few hopes, much love, and many prayers. A widow's letter tells me, that her only child fell at Iuka; and a father's, that his eldest son died before Dalton. "What wonder," each letter asks, "that I wish to die and be at rest?" Among so many, of course a love-letter can be found, breathing a first avowal. It is written to some village beauty, and hints at rivals, and her sometime smiles and sometime frowns. The village beauty is, I judge, a slight coquette, who has led her lover along with little encouragements and little rebuffs. His letter is written in a manly strain, and tells her that he had hoped to gain an honorable name, and come back to win her in an early peace. But the peace has not come. He can bear this suspense no longer. He begs her to deal frankly and truly with him, and, if she loves him, *to answer this letter.* The letter will never be answered! I laid it away, and thought that I would send it, by some flag of truce, to the unknown belle. But my papers were captured, and this letter, on which so many hopes hung, was lost.

The threatening trouble drew nearer. There were frequent alarms—the cannon rung out their warnings often during the night—the long rolls were beaten and the troops assembled and stood on their arms. One night I awoke at the call of the cannon near my window, and heard the men assembling and the ammunition wagons rolling past. To one accustomed to act at such times, such forced inaction is the severest of trials. I watched from habit, expecting the rattling small arms of an attack, but the night wore away in unusual silence. The next morning I was told that all our troops save the sick and a few on guard, had gone. The sick men whispered each other that we were defenceless, and it was well that we had the telegraph and railroad, and could call our troops back in case of an attack from across the river. A few hours passed and then the telegraph suddenly ceased its ticking—the railroad was cut and the enemy was between us and our forces at La Fourche.

No relief came, and after three days of suspense, Brashear was carried by assault. Some of our sick men formed a line and behaved well, but they were quickly overpowered. The red flag of our hospital was not understood by the assaulting party, and for a little while it looked as if no quarter would be given by the Wild Texans to our sick and wounded. I had risen and mounted my horse after the attack commenced, and I now dismounted at the hospital, and with Captain Noblet of the 1st Indiana Artillery stood awaiting the result. The Captain was full of wrath, and vowed that he would put the two or three charges, still in his revolver, in places where two or three of the murdering villains would feel them. A wild looking squad, with broad hats and jangling spurs, rushed, revolver in hand, upon the building. In no very decided mood at the time, and acting chiefly from the military habit of looking to some one in authority, I asked sharply if there was an officer among them. They stopped, looked, a trifle disconcerted, and one answered that he was a sergeant.

"This is a hospital," I said, authoritatively. "Sergeant, put two men on guard at the door, and don't let any but the wounded pass in."

"Well then, Bill," said the sergeant, "you and John stand guard here. And now see you don't let nobody go in unless they be wounded."

This was the first and last order I ever gave to a Confederate soldier, and it is due to the sergeant to say that he executed it promptly and well.

About the same instant another squad rushed to a side window and poked their rifles through the sash. Dr. Willets, the surgeon of the 176th, at the moment was operating on a wounded soldier. With professional coolness he turned to the window, and in the decided manner that one would speak to a crowd of small boys, said—

"This is a hospital; you mustn't come here. Go away from the window and get out of my light."

The rifles were withdrawn; the party looked at the window a moment in a somewhat awe-struck manner, and then saying to each other, "You mustn't go there," they withdrew.

The wounded of both sides were brought in, and our

surgeons, with scrupulous impartiality, treated all alike. From beside their operating table I was moved to an upper room with Lieutenant Stevenson of the 176th. A minnie ball had torn through the entire length of his foot, leaving a frightful wound that threatened lockjaw and amputation. On the next cot lay a wounded Confederate named Lewis—a plain, simple-hearted man, who, for the next week, proved a useful and trustworthy friend. As we thus lay there, my regimental colors, by some strange chance, were brought into the room. Our conversation stopped — the sick and wounded raised themselves from their cots, and all eyes were fastened upon the inanimate flag as though it were a being of intelligence and life. The Texan soldier first broke the silence.

"That," he said, in a dreamy way—half to himself and half to us—"that has been the proudest flag that ever floated."

"*And is still, sir,*" said my wounded lieutenant, proudly.

The Texan said nothing. I expected an outbreak, for there had been no little defiance in the lieutenant's reply, but none came. Some old emotion had evidently touched his heart and carried him back to earlier and better days.

As he turned away my color-sergeant whispered to me a plan for destroying the colors, which, however, I did not approve. He pleaded that he knew every thread of that flag, and that it would almost kill him to see it borne away by rebel hands. "No, Sergeant," I was obliged to reply, "we must keep our colors by fighting for them, and not by a dirty trick." The answer satisfied neither the sergeant nor my fellow officers. Yet before my own imprisonment was over, I had the great happiness of learning that the undestroyed flag, honorably recaptured, was restored to its regiment.

An officer soon appeared charged with the duty of paroling our men. His quiet and courteous manner said plainly that he was a gentleman, and he introduced himself as Captain Watt, of Gen. Mouton's staff. The Captain and I looked at each other as men do who think they have met before. He then informed me that formerly he had spent his summers at Saratoga and Newport, and that he thought we must have known each other there. For this slight reason—so slight that many men would have made it a good excuse for dropping an acquaintance, if any had existed—Captain Watt called on me repeatedly, procured an order for my being retained in the Brashear hospital, and for several months carefully transmitted to me such letters as found their way through the lines. His family had been one of the wealthiest in New Orleans, and were now refugees in Europe. He had entered the army under the belief that it was a duty to his State, and on the capture of the city had beheld the ruin of all who were dearest to him. Yet he made no ill-timed allusions to this, and in our conversations always selected pleasant topics and spoke kindly of the hours he had spent and the acquaintances he had made in the North.

The chief Confederate surgeon (Dr. Hughes, of Victoria, Texas,) next arrived, and assumed command at the hospital. It caused at first but little change. Our own surgeons continued in charge of our wounded—our steward continued to dispense the stores, and the stores continued to be forthcoming. The Confederate surgeons were polite and kind, doing all they could to make us comfortable, and expressing thanks for the treatment previously bestowed on their own wounded. Thus, in a few hours, our affairs had settled down in their new channels; and we, with a strange, new feeling of restriction upon us, set ourselves to wait for the bad news, and fresh reverses likely to come. From our window we could see the Confederate forces crossing the river. They waited not for tardy quarter-masters or proper transportation, but, in flat boats and dug-outs, pressed steadily across. A little steamer dropped out of one of the narrow bayous, and worked ceaselessly, bringing over artillery. Ere sunset, we estimated that five thousand men and four batteries had crossed, and were moving forward to break our communications on the Mississippi, and compel us to raise the siege of Port Hudson.

From this early day, there was a strong resolve in the minds of most of us, to be cheerful before the enemy, and, whatever we felt, not to let them see us downcast. When the mind is really roused and in motion, a little effort will turn it into almost any channel. We made the effort, and succeeded. One individual who came in last, and ventured to say, with solemn visage, that this calamity was awful, was immediately frowned down, and warned that, if he talked such nonsense here, he should be moved to some other ward. The effect was magical, and in ten minutes he became rather a merry, careless kind of fellow. This treatment, I believe, saved many lives; and I found that my own convalescence, which had been slow and changeful in the previous quiet, was now rapid and steady.

There were sorrows enough to see, if one chose to look toward them. So many causes never united to depress, and never produced so little effect. Neither the shameful loss of the post, nor the presence of the sick and wounded filling every room, nor our unburied dead who lay around the building, nor the prospect of a long captivity, nor the helplessness of disease, nor the suffering of wounds, were sufficient to make us appear sad. I marvelled then, and cannot understand now, how the mind was able to throw off these troubles, and how *real* this enforced cheerfulness became. A sense of duty dictated it at the beginning, and redeemed it from heartlessness afterward. Once, indeed, my spirits failed me, as I searched some private letters to find an address. They were so light-hearted and happy, and dwelt on the belief, as on a certainty, that he, to whom they were written, would return crowned with honor. It was a happy and brief illusion. An only sister had given her only brother to the war—the orphan pair had made this great sacrifice of separation; and now I had to write to the young girl, and say that he had been my most trusted officer, and had fallen for the honor of his flag.*

There was a class of captives who saw the loss of Brashear with heavier hearts than those who possessed the rights and hopes of "prisoners of war." The unhappy contrabands were agitated before the blow fell, but met it with the tearless apathy of their race. "The niggers don't look as if they wanted to see us," I heard one Confederate soldier say to another.

"No," said the other; "but you'll see a herd of fat planters here to-morrow after them. *They* don't fight any, but they are always on hand for their niggers."

It was even so: for days, planter after planter appeared, and party after party of men, women and children, laden with their beds and baggage, tramped sorrowfully past our quarters. The hundreds that remained went, I know not whither.

There was one woman, a quadroon, who had been an attendant in our hospital. With her there were an old mother, darker than herself, and a little daughter so fair, that no one ever suspected her of being tainted with the blood of the hapless race. This woman, through all the turmoil and trial of that time, never lost the little marks of neatness and propriety that tell so plainly in woman of innate dignity and refinement. The tasteful simplicity of her frequently changed dress; the neat collar and snowy cuffs; the pretty work-box, and more especially her quiet reserve, indicated rather the lady

* Captain John S. Cutter.

than the slave. During the fight she had been calm and brave, and when a couple of cowards had rushed into the hospital and begged for a place where they could lie down and hide themselves, this *woman*, while volleys were firing at the hospital, and men and women falling in the passages, had shown these *men* to a room and closed the door on them, and walked away so quietly that one might have thought her beyond the reach of the danger that threatened them. An hour or two later, as she passed through the ward where we lay, she stopped at the window and looked out on the scene of the Confederates crossing the river. Of all the persons to whom the capture of Brashear boded grief and wrong, there probably was not one to whom it threatened so much as to her. With her mother and her child, she had been preparing to seek the surer refuge of the North, and this direful calamity had come when the place of safety appeared almost within her reach. Yet she shed no tears, and uttered no complainings. Her large, sad eyes fastened on the river, she stood beside the window and heard the shouts and yells that told of the Confederate triumph. For half an hour she never moved; her face retained its soft composure, and only once the muscles of the lip fluttered and trembled, as though there might be a troubled sea within. Then she turned and went back to her work, as calmly as if she alone had suffered no change. She cheered those men who were struggling for strength to go out on parole; she worked for those officers who were to be sent forward into captivity. For herself, she never invited aid or sympathy. We asked her if we might not send for her former master to come and take her back to her old home. But this, for some untold reason, she steadfastly refused. It was urged that she and her child would be sent far into Texas or Arkansas; and that they might be seized, as so much booty, by some of these half-savage strangers. She answered quietly, that she had thought of this. Ere we parted, we asked her what future help we could give, and what plan she would pursue to regain her freedom, or secure some less dangerous home. And she said briefly, that she did not know, and said no more.

The captured officers, able to march, were sent forward to Shreveport, and the men were paroled and marched off to our lines. Three officers of my regiment remained with me—two sick, and one severely wounded. Two "citizen prisoners" were also added to our number. One of these, whom I shall call Mr. Stratford, was held as lessee of a confiscated plantation. His wife was permitted to remain with him, and she now visited the hospital daily. The other civilian was Mr. Dwight Parce, of Chenango County, New York, who had just begun business in Brashear. He now witnessed the destruction of his property with undiminished cheerfulness, and, although an invalid, fated to fill a prisoner's grave in Texas, met the discomforts that awaited him with a serenity and hopefulness that nothing ever disturbed.

We all effected some captures of baggage. Captain

Watt sent me an order for the delivery of mine if it could be found, and Dr. Hughes, with ever ready kindness, advised me to take his ambulance and search for it at the fort, where some captured property was stored. The guard consisted of a young gentleman in his shirt sleeves and no shoes, who, when requested to go, whistled violently, and perched himself on the rear of the ambulance, with his face toward the hospital and his back toward me. I asked him, with some surprise, if he was not going to take his rifle; at which he stopped whistling and said, he reckoned not. After whistling a few minutes, he further defined his position by saying, that if I ran away he reckoned he could run after me; and then, that he reckoned the climate had been a heap too much for me. After another whistle his stiffness wore away a trifle, and he manifestly tried to put me at my ease by saying, "Dog gone the Lousanny climate, and the bayous, and the beef; and dog gone the Lousanyans, they're the meanest set of people ever I see. I'd just as soon shoot one of 'em as a Yank." This put me quite at my ease, and we then had a very interesting conversation. The etymology of "dog gone" my guard was ignorant of; he suggested that it meant pretty much what something else did, but wasn't quite so bad, in which opinion I coincided. Since then I have learnt that this expressive phrase is derived from the threat of putting a *dog on* you, and that it saves annually, in Texas, an immense amount of swearing, and is found to answer just as well.

On the morning of the third of July, the Officer of the Day appeared. He was a Captain in Colonel Bates' Texan Battalion, and he blandly begged that we would prepare to move in the afternoon; the boat would be ready at five, and we would be sent to the hospital at Franklin, where we would be much more comfortable. The boat did not come, however, and we remained to celebrate the "Fourth" at Brashear. We went round among our sick men who remained, to cheer them with the certainty of their early release; we read the Declaration, and we drank a bottle of wine, which Mrs. Stratford, with patriotic devotion, smuggled in for us. Our friend, the ex-officer of the day, reappeared to apologize; the boat had been detained—he knew he must have caused us much trouble—he had come to beg us to forgive him—he deeply regretted that he had not known of the delay in time to inform us. To-day he believed that there would be no delay, and he had just requested the new Officer to order the boat up to the hospital, so that we should not have the trouble of walking down to where she lay. Nothing could have been more elegant, chivalric, and delightful. If he were one of my own officers and I were the Lieutenant-General, he could not have been more courteous and respectful.

We started on our "Fourth of July excursion" in the afternoon. While the boat was lying at the wharf, an officer, with long white hair and of imposing appearance, came slowly down the saloon. As he drew near I observed a Colonel's insignia on his collar, and one of the guard whispered me, that it was Colonel Bates, the commanding officer at Brashear. The Colonel marched up to me, extended his hand, and with grand solemnity, in keeping with his dignified bearing, said:

"Colonel, I have come down now to apologize for not having waited upon you before. I ought to have done so, sir—I ought to have done so. But I have been over-occupied. I pray you to excuse me, sir."

When I consider our difference in years, and the different circumstances that surrounded each, I do not know of any incident that could have pleased me more than this stately courtesy of the old Colonel. An interesting conversation followed, in which I learnt that he was an Alabamian by birth. He spoke highly of the Texan character, which, he said, excelled in bravery and simplicity; but he warned me that the country could furnish few comforts, such, he said, as Northerners have at home. Then, when the boat was ready to start, he called up the officer of the guard, and said to him:

"Captain, your orders are strict, I know; but these gentlemen are invalids; they are too weak to escape, sir. You must construe your orders liberally, sir, in favor of the sick. Do not let the guard trouble these gentlemen, and make them as comfortable as you can."

There was another Colonel who succeeded Colonel Bates, at Brashear; he was a citizen of a New England State, and had been an ice merchant in New Orleans. When the war came, he went, not "with his State" but with his property. All the indignities, ill-treatment, meanness and cruelty that we met with at Brashear and Franklin, came directly from him. While the *real* Southern officers were showing us unsought kindness and attention—while they were overlooking what they sincerely believed to be the needless ruin of their homes, and the wanton destruction of their property, this miserable Northern renegade was bullying Northern ladies —"bucking and gagging" unfortunate prisoners, and sending sick and wounded officers out of the hospital by orders as cowardly as they were cruel.

The Franklin Hospital had been the "Franklin House" before the war, and stood close beside the bayou. Lieutenant Stevenson was placed in the wounded ward, and the rest of us were assigned three pleasant rooms in a wing of the building. Our guard consisted of a corporal, named Ingram, and six men of Colonel Bates' regiment. They bivouacked on the piazza, and completed our confusion as to what Wild Texans are. They did not drink; they did not swear; they did not gamble. They were watchful of us, but did everything kindly and with a willingness that greatly lessened our feeling of dependence.

The surgeon in charge of the hospital, Dr. Marten, was polite and kind. A stylish little French lieutenant of the 10th Louisiana, named Solomon, was assiduous in his attentions. He detailed a contraband as our especial servant; hourly sent us little presents, in the way of fruit and refreshments, and paid us those easy, chatty visits, that Frenchmen pay so much better than any other men. There was a sort of Dutch Major-Domo, one Schneider, who took us under his special protection, blowing up the cook and scolding the waiter, on our behalf, a dozen times a day. There was also a sergeant of the Crescent regiment—a soldier and disciplinarian, but easy and communicative toward us. Lastly, there was our contraband, bearing the name of Ben, and very sharp and shrewd was he, and never wanting in good-humor or flourishing obeisances.

The ladies of Franklin flocked to the hospital, bringing fruit and flowers, and knick-knacks of their own preparing. They differed considerably with the doctors on questions of diet; and did about as much damage, in their pretty way, as patriotic young ladies have done in other than Confederate hospitals. They carefully avoided the cot of the solitary Yankee prisoner in the wounded ward; the well-bred passing it by as though the slight were casual, and the ill-bred, showing with studied care, that it was intentional. The Wild Texans who had captured us shared not in these patriotic manifestations. They, on the contrary, divided with Lieutenant Stevenson whatever they received, looked after him as though he were a brother soldier, and, once or twice, asked their fair visitors rather angrily, why they didn't give this or that to that gentleman on the fourth cot. Yet it must not be supposed that this conduct of the Franklin fair proceeded entirely from their own wicked imaginings. The women, like the men of the South, are all slaves of public opinion. After awhile one lady, giving way to the natural kindness of her nature, stopped at the prisoner's cot, and then the others followed the example. The presents flowed in with a free hand, and the sails once fairly round on this tack, the wind seemed to blow as strongly from the chivalric quarter as it had previously blown from the patriotic.

This narrative would not be truthful if I omitted therefrom a statement of the fare, during our fortnight in the Franklin hospital. It was so much better than I had expected; so much better than I had supposed it possible that prisoners could receive at rebel hands; so different from the fare which we knew was to follow, that I carefully noted down the bill on several days, and from these select a favorable specimen.

" *Wednesday, July* 15. At Sunrise.—French Coffee and Biscuits.

"Breakfast.—Beef Steak, Beef Stew, Cucumbers, Stewed Peaches, Melons, French Bread, Biscuits, Toast and Tea.

"Dinner.—Soup, Roast Beef, Beef *a la mode*, Cucumbers, Egg Plant, Lima Beans, French Bread, Biscuits, Tea."

This easy prison-life, however, received a jog, in the shape of an officer of Speight's Battalion of Texas Cavalry. He was introduced to us as Lieutenant Geo. C. Duncan, and he bore orders to carry us to Niblett's Bluff, on the Sabine. It appeared therefrom that we were to be moved to the southern side of Texas, and not to follow the officers captured with us.

The orders were, to carry *all* the prisoners at the hospital to Niblett's Bluff; but when the officer saw Lieutenant Stevenson, and heard the surgeon's statement, he sent down a special report from the surgeon, and waited for further orders. In the meanwhile, our polite French friend, Lieutenant Solomon, drove Mrs. Stratford to New Iberia, and we awaited, with some anxiety, our departure, and discussed the probabilities of marching through, or giving out by the way.

IV.

THE MARCH.

It was Sunday morning, about sunrise, when Lieutenant Duncan appeared at the door, and informed us that we must start immediately. There was an instantaneous springing up—a hurried toilet—a rapid rolling of blankets, and a hastily-snatched breakfast of bread and coffee. I remarked, with more unconcern in my manner than I really felt, that I supposed Lieutenant Stevenson would remain. The lieutenant's countenance fell, and, looking another way, he said, nervously, "Orders have come to move *all* immediately, and I have no alternative." It was my unpleasant task, therefore, to go down and announce to the wounded officer that he must go. In addition to his painful wound, he was suffering from an attack of fever. His exhausted appearance frightened me, though I talked quite boldly of the good effects of change of air, and the advantages of continuing with us.

A clumsy plantation wagon rumbled to the door, and the new guard, mounted on wild-looking Texan horses, drew up around it. The old guard, like good fellows, helped us quite cordially in carrying out our baggage; and they shook hands and bade us good bye, with a warmth that savored much less of rebel enemies than of countrymen and friends. Some newly arrived prisoners were brought from the Court House, and we started. As we moved off, one of them seized me by the hand with many expressions of surprise. At first I did not recognize him, but, after a moment, discovered that he was Captain Frederick Van Tine, of my former regiment, and learnt that he, with two Massachusetts officers, was captured on the Mississippi, and, for the last week, had been confined in the jail at Thiboudeau.

Up the main street of Franklin we marched two by two, the guard strung along on each side, their rifles unslung and their eyes watching us, as if they somewhat feared an immediate escape. The loafers of Franklin of course turned out to stare at us, and made remarks rarely complimentary; the women looked at us from the door-steps as we passed, some triumphantly, and a few in pity. At the head of this inglorious procession it was my place to walk; but the new prisoners revealed the hitherto concealed news, and I felt proud and happy over the long delayed result of Vicksburg and Port Hudson.

Beside our own party, and the three officers from the Mississippi, were a number of "citizen prisoners," and and unfortunate deserter whom they had caught at Brashear. Of these civilians, a dozen were Irishmen, and they immediately placed themselves at the head of the column, and proceeded to walk and talk with a zeal that nobody attempted to equal. A move is always animating, even when it is toward captivity; but our excitement was short-lived. Hardly had we passed from the shadow of the town, when the convalescents felt the effect of the burning, fever-kindling sun. It was a serious business for some of us. One hundred and eighty miles distant flowed the Sabine, and we were to march there, over open prairies and in the middle of the Southern summer.

Before a mile was travelled over, I could see the effect of the fearful heat in others, and feel it on myself. Faces grew flushed; coats were stripped off, and the perspiration poured in streams. Yet it was a matter of honor not to give up. For my own part, I was smarting with mortification at the disgrace of Brashear, and resolved, and re-resolved, to walk till I fell dead, before one of these Southern soldiers should say that a Yankee Colonel had given out.

At the head of the guard rode a good-looking young fellow, tall and sinewy, and with the merriest face I have ever seen in a Southerner. I had some doubts, at first, whether he was a private or a Captain, but found that he was a corporal. He was mounted on a compact little bay, called, in Texas, a pony; a long revolver was stuck in his belt; a lariat rope loosely coiled hung on the saddle-bow; his bright Springfield rifle was balanced across the pommel, and with his broad hat and heavy, jangling Spanish spurs, he formed a brilliant picture of a Wild Texan. As some little changes and arrangements were wanting and the lieutenant was not in sight, I addressed myself to the corporal, and asked if he would order a halt for a moment. "Why to be sure I will," was his very ready reply, followed up with the order, "Now, halt here, men, and let these prisoners put their little tricks on the wagon; there is no need of their packing them."

We took advantage of the halt to lash some sticks to the sides of the wagon and to spread upon them our blankets, so as to form an awning over Lieutenant Stevenson. But the sun beat down hotter and hotter. At the next halt, one of us took a canteen from the end of the wagon—the water was hot, so incredibly hot that the others were called up to feel it, and all agreed that its heat was painful. My first impression was, that this intense burning heat would blister us. But the damp Louisiana atmosphere caused floods of perspiration, pouring over the exposed face and hands, and soaking quickly through every garment. Faces grew more and more flushed; conversation flagged and soon ceased. Those who, at the beginning, rattled away cheerfully, walked in moody silence near each other, occasionally exchanging distressed looks, but rarely, if ever, speaking a word.

About mid-day the expected shower of the rainy season came down on us furiously. We drew up under some trees, and stood close against the leeward side of their trunks, until it blew over. The different characteristics of the three parties who were gathered there immediately developed. The Irishmen laughed, hullabaloed, pushed each other out in the rain, and treated the affair as a capital joke. The Northerners shifted their positions, and attempted improvements, while the rain was at the worst—grumbled a great deal, and hurled fierce denunciations at, what they called, their "luck." The Southerners silently unrolled their blankets, folded them around their shoulders, looked upward at the storm with their usual sad indifference of expression, made no attempts to better their condition, and waited apathetically till it was over.

A prairie spread out for several miles immediately beyond our sheltering trees, and the road curved around its outskirts. It was a prairie, but a tame one; interspersed with fields; pastured by cattle; surrounded by houses, and looking like any dull, uninteresting plain. Its grass, however, was thick and wet, and its sticky black mud soon loaded our boots and almost glued us fast. The coolness of the air quickly vanished, and the sun, more burning than ever, re-appeared. We dragged on wearily, very wearily, casting wistful glances at the grove on the other side, which rose very slowly, and, for a long time, seemed as distant as when we started. At last, however, we manifestly drew nearer; the chimneys of a house could be distinguished in the foliage, and the guard cheered us with the assurance that it was the house at which we were to halt. Every one made a last effort, and after half an hour's exertion, we dragged ourselves out of the muddy prairie and into a plantation yard, bordering on the Teche.

We sat there waiting for the wagon, and watching a

small drove of hogs that had come down the bank of the bayou, and, half immersed, were greedily eating the green scum that covered the water. The lieutenant had bought provisions at the house, and hired the contrabands to cook for us. The dinner finally appeared, consisting of a large kettle of boiled beef, and a quantity of corn bread in the shape of little rolls. It did not impress us favorably; but the guard seemed to think it excellent—perhaps because *boiled* beef was a rarity—perhaps because the corn bread was a superior article, (I was not a judge of it then); and one, with charming simplicity, said, "If we do as well as *this*, it *will* do!" To which rhapsody one of my disgusted friends was obliged to respond, with a faint and sickly smile, "Yes, yes; it is very nice."

The place of bivouac that night was in the grass-covered yard, or rather field, of one of the finest plantations on the Teche. The owner soon appeared, accompanied by his son, his son-in-law, and a friend. He was an old gentleman, dressed with the scrupulous taste and neatness of a Frenchman, and treated us with as much politeness and as little kindness as could very well be united. The son-in-law regaled us with a description of the manner in which some of our troops had plundered his house, and burnt his furniture; and the friend sat himself down, and opened with the invariable remark, "We consider this a *most* unnatural war, sir;" which he followed up with the invariable question, "When do you think there will be peace, sir?" To these I gave my invariable replies, that we also thought it a most unnatural war, and that there would be peace whenever the Southern soldiers chose to go home and take care of their own affairs. The gentleman seemed very much disgusted at the idea of having peace on such simple and easy terms, and said solemnly, that he couldn't allow himself to believe it.

There was a large open shed beside us, but the ground was covered with fleas, and we preferred the wet grass and heavy dew of a Louisiana night, to these pests of a tropical climate. But few slept well. For a long time I felt too tired to close my eyes, and awoke repeatedly, aching in every part. When daylight dawned we rose so stiff and sore that we could hardly move, and with renewed apprehensions made ready for another day. Lieutenant Stevenson showed such increased exhaustion that the Confederate officer took me aside and said, that he would not be guilty of carrying him beyond New Iberia.

We started, not at daylight, as was intended, but a long time after the sun was up. With all such parties there are many petty causes of delay, and it requires an iron-handed commander to bear them down, and carry his party off at the appointed hour. Lieutenant Duncan was too good-natured for this, and instead of coercing us, he, on the contrary, told us to choose our own time, and not to start till we were ready. The delay brought down the burning sun again upon us, and the pain and weariness of this second day much exceeded those of the first.

As we thus toiled along, the road, which was running between uninclosed fields, approached a tall rail fence. Three or four of us were walking a few yards in advance of the guard, when we heard the corporal shout from behind, "Take care of the bull! Take care of the bull!" I looked ahead and saw nothing very alarming: a large red bull was drawing himself up, and lashing his sides with his tail. After a moment or two, however, he started toward us, shaking his head and breaking into a low, deep bellow. He was a magnificent animal, with long, low, spreading horns, and moved in a full, square trot that many a horse might envy. There was a scramble at once for the fence which stood very nearly midway between us and the bull. What the result might have been I think somewhat doubtful, had not the gallant corporal, on his bright little bay, rushed past us on a gallop. The pony was a herding pony and understood his business. Like a spirited dog, he flew straight at the bull until they nearly touched, then wheeling he kept alongside, watching him closely and sheering off whenever the long horns made a lunge toward himself. The pony did this of his own accord, for, as he wheeled, his rider held the rifle in his left hand and was drawing the long revolver with his right, and these Texan horses are rarely taught to wheel from the pressure of the leg. A finer picture of intelligent instinct than this pony presented could hardly be painted: his ears erect, his eyes flashing, and his whole soul in the chase. The corporal was not slower than his horse. He brought the long revolver up; a shot flashed, and the poor beast received a heavy wound. This diverted his attention from us, for, with a loud bellow, he wheeled toward the corporal. But the pony's eye was on him, and, quicker than spur or rein could make him, he also wheeled, and scoured off across the plain faster than any bull could go. The corporal brought up the rifle, and there was a second flash —a second wound, for the bull staggered, and then walked slowly and proudly away. Occasionally he stopped, turned defiantly round, uttered deep bellowings, and shook at us his splendid horns.

The incident afforded us a little excitement, and led me into a conversation with the corporal, who narrated anecdotes of the wonderful intelligence of herding ponies. The heat, the dust, the glaring sun, and increasing pain and weariness at length stopped even a conversation on so interesting a topic as horses are and ever will be, and I was fain to drag myself along without expending an ounce of strength on any object beyond the dusty road. We entered upon the last two miles, and saw Iberia in the distance. The road ran between hedges twenty feet high—it was filled with a long column of dust—not a breath of outer air disturbed it, and the sun shone directly down from his noon-day height. I felt myself grow weaker and weaker as we advanced through this green boiler. The perspiration poured into my eyes and blinded me—my head whirled round—my feet stumbled and dragged, so that every step seemed almost the last. While in this critical state, a couple of pretty Louisiana "young ladies" stopped their carriage, and greatly refreshed me by expressing the hope that we should be hung at the end of the lane, and the opinion that hanging was quite as good treatment as nigger-thieves deserved. Such was the power of this well-timed stimulus, that I kept on for more than a mile, and at last found that I was in the midst of the little town of New Iberia.

We halted in the shade of some large trees. There seemed to be an unusual number of vagabonds in New Iberia, who congregated closely round us, and asked impudent questions (generally as to how we liked the war *now*), until it occurred to our guards that this might be annoying to us, and then they very promptly drove the Iberian loafers back. One cowardly-looking, black-eyed little rascal, however, was very desirous of finding an officer of the Twenty-first Indiana amongst us that he might kill him, and repeatedly hinted that he had a great mind to kill one of us anyhow. But one of the guard quieted him by the suggestion that if he wanted to kill a Yank, he'd find plenty of them over on the Mississippi, and that he'd better go there instead of skulking round in the rear—anyhow, he'd better stop insulting prisoners, or he'd have a right smart chance to kill a *Texan*—dog-goned if he wouldn't.

Soon after this, an officer of the Provost Guard appeared. The roll of the "citizen prisoners" was called over, and all but six marched off to the jail. We were put in motion, and marched to the outskirts of the town, where we halted beside a saw-mill standing on the bank of the Teche. The lieutenant then brought a surgeon, who speedily pronounced in favor of receiving Lieutenant Stevenson, and directed that he should be taken at once to his hospital.

During the afternoon, our kind and courteous French friend, Lieutenant Solomon, appeared, to take us to the hospital, and thence to his own house. I asked Lieutenant Duncan for a guard, and he politely sent one of his men with us. One of my officers walked with me to the hospital. It was in a church, and at its extreme end we found Lieutenant Stevenson. He looked wretched, and my hopes sank as I saw him. The church was crowded with Confederate sick, and he was the only prisoner there. Yet there was no alternative. We knew that if he were carried along, a sadder parting would soon ensue. Faintly hoping that we should again see him, and inwardly praying that he might find the friends he sorely needed, we bade him farewell.

The French lieutenant rejoined us in the street, and led the way to his own house. He wished, he said, to present us to Madame, and offer us some slight refreshment, which was not good, but was better than we might enjoy again. We soon reached his house, and were presented to Madame, who received us with the grace and politeness of a French lady. The slight refreshment, doubtless, was preparing, and we were comfortably waiting to enjoy it, when a patriot soldier of the Confederacy, with the villainous look peculiar to those of Louisiana, stuck his gun and then his head in the room, and said sulkily, that the Provost Marshal wanted us. Our worthy lieutenant accompanied us, saying, "Oh, surely it must be a mistake; somebody has told him you are making an escape. He will let you return to my house, and you shall stay all the afternoon." Arrived at the Provost Marshal's, the Louisiana patriot left us on the sidewalk, and stepped in to inform the august official that we were in waiting. That magnate immediately came forth—a youthful, swarthy, small-sized, unwashed Louisianian, with a consequential air, and a vagabond face. "Take these fellows back to your camp," he said, addressing our Texan guard. "I won't have prisoners running about my town." As he said this, he honored us with a vicious stare, and then banged back into his office.

There was no resisting this eloquence, so back we went. Our guard, who had been very silent, became very talkative. He swore pardonable oaths at the Louisianians in general, and the Provost Marshal in particular. As to the former, he said they were all a disgrace to the South; and as to the latter, that if ever he got a chance, he'd scalp *him*—dog-gone if he wouldn't. In camp, his excitement extended to the rest. Our gallant friend, the corporal, was especially indignant.

"What," he said, "he spoke so right before you, without your having insulted him. The dog-gone little puppy. If I'd been there, I'd have slapped his face, and then run for Texas. There's just such ducks everywhere, and most of all in Louisiana. Dog-gone them—I'd like to shoot the whole of them."

Our wounded honor being soothed by these chivalric

sentiments, and a shower of rain coming up about the same time, we retired to the saw-mill, where we selected soft planks, swept away the saw-dust, and made ready for the night. About dark, Lieutenant Duncan returned, with anger and mortification glowing in his face. He had not been able to get fresh mules or a good wagon, or full rations, or even a wagon cover, *for prisoners*, and he was vexed and wrathful at the refusals he had met. "I tell you what it is, though, gentlemen," he said, "you shall be taken care of, and have the best this country can give you, if I take it out of their houses with my revolver. It's not so in Texas, gentlemen. There our people haven't got much, but they will give you what they have." In fact, the good lieutenant was so chagrined and mortified, that I had to assure him that we were not children, and would rather undergo a little extra hardship, than put him to further trouble. But while affairs were gliding in this harmonious and humane channel within the saw-mill, some wicked imp suggested to our friend, the Provost Marshal, the feasibility of his bestowing on us another kick. Hardly had the lieutenant wiped the perspiration from his brow, and looked around for a dry plank on which to sleep, when a second Louisiana patriot, dirtier even than the first, appeared. He delivered an order to the lieutenant. It was to pack up and be off instantly—he, the Provost Marshal, wouldn't have prisoners camping in his town over night.

We accordingly packed up and went off, not more than a hundred yards (for the saw-mill was on the boundary of the town), and stopped at an abandoned barn, just beyond the Provost Marshal's jurisdiction. The barn was dirty—the ground around it muddy—the fleas were hale and hearty—and these little circumstances added a great deal of force to the thanks which the guard lavished on the Provost Marshal. Yet we looked forward with hopefulness to the morrow, for then we were to turn off from the Teche, and leaving civilization and the hateful Louisianians behind us, strike off, undisturbed, on the free prairies.

V.

THE PRAIRIES.

The road ran, for several miles, between hedges and among plantations, and close to gardens and houses, with their fields and fences, until it suddenly emerged on a broad, unbounded prairie. Our guards' eyes sparkled when they saw it, and they declared that this began to look like Texas. We all felt better at the sight, and the fresh breeze that swept over it almost swept away the weary weakness of the previous days. There is a profound sense of loneliness and littleness on these great seas of green far exceeding that which men feel in forests. There is such an absence of *objects*—such long distances appearing to the eye, and before which the feet grow feeble—such a want of all shelter and protection, that one wishes for the woods, and acknowledges a companionship in hills and trees beyond all that he has ever known before.

A long noon-day halt was made at a Frenchman's, whose wretched shanty stood environed by a beautiful grove of the deep-shading China tree; and, during the afternoon, we found the prairie interspersed with small plantations. These took away the sense of loneliness, and, in some respects, added to the interest of the march. There was a good stiff breeze, too, blowing directly from the west, (to which we travelled) and all moved cheerfully along, shaking off fatigue and forgetting, for the time, that we were prisoners. As the sun approached his setting, we descended by a gently sloping plain toward a wood that marks and hides Vermillion Bayou. While it was still a mile or two distant, we turned from the wagon-trail and made our way across the prairie to a plantation, whose large white house and numerous out-buildings peered forth from a grove of overhanging trees.

The plantation was owned by a lady, who kindly allowed her servants to cook our supper, and gave us her lawn to bivouac upon. She also invited Mr. and Mrs. Stratford to occupy a room in her house, and showed the rare good taste and delicacy of not coming out to stare at us. We found ourselves still connected with civilized life; for supper was spread out handsomely in the dining-room, and was accompanied by the luxury of real French coffee, served in delicate china.

We started earlier than usual the next morning, and soon crossed the strip of prairie between us and the Vermillion. The belt of wood was not more than half a mile in breadth, and near its farther edge we found a narrow, sluggish stream, almost bridged by the ferry-scow, yet deep in mud, and with miry banks that made it difficult to cross. As we waited for the wagon that was slowly rumbling along, we discovered below the ferry, closely drawn up against the bank and almost hidden by the trees, a full rigged schooner, that had eluded the watchfulness of our blockaders, and escaped the eyes of our cavalry, and now lay snugly waiting for the proper time to glide down the bayou and escape on the open sea.

The wagon rolled up while we were scanning and discussing the little blockade runner, and we began our crossing. It was not a labor of very great importance, for when one end of the scow had been pushed a few feet from the eastern bank, the other end ran into the western. We found the latter much higher than the former, being, in Southern phrase, "something of a bluff." On mounting it, we saw a rolling prairie spreading out like a lake of green, and enclosed by distant woods which seemed its shore. The "timber," (as forests in the West are called,) was four or five miles distant on either side, and, to the front of us, sank down behind the far-off horizon. Numerous herds were in sight; and troops of young cattle would draw up and stare at us. They were not the "fine stock" of our good breeders; yet, still were beautiful creatures—straight-backed, fine-boned, and with heads gracefully carried and erect. When our shouts startled them into motion, they carried themselves off with the same high horse-like trot I had been struck with in our bull on the Teche, and then, breaking into an easy gallop, bounded away like deer. The guards repeatedly warned us to keep near the horsemen, and said, that these cattle of the prairies did not know what a man afoot was, and were so wild that they would attack us if we ventured near them.

The guard had been improving daily since we left Franklin. No formal parole was given by us, yet there was an informal one which we respected, and in which they placed implicit confidence. They behaved, too, with great kindness, constantly dismounting and making first one and then another of us ride. Our column broke up into little parties of twos and threes, the faster walkers opening gaps on those who took it more leisurely, and each one travelling at whatever rate he best liked. After five or six miles of this, three of us, with a like number of the guard, reached a little house that stood alone in the prairie. The guards showed their appreciation of our honor, by handing us their horses and rifles to take care of while they went into the house. After a while they returned, and showed their appreciation of our appetites by bringing us a pail full of milk for a drink.

We watched the different parties that dotted the prairie for a mile or two behind us, until they severally came up, wiping the perspiration from their faces and throwing themselves on the grass beside us. The wagon overtook us last, and then we rose and resumed the march. The prairie continued to present the same rich picture of beautiful seclusion. Occasionally its timber-shores approached each other, and sometimes they opened into successive lakes. Yet, with all this beauty, we found ourselves becoming hot and weary. There were no way-side trees to cast an occasional shade, and no brooks or springs at which to halt and re-fill canteens. The usual morning breeze that sweeps across the prairies, as across the sea, went down, and wistful eyes were thrown at a distant plantation which we saw embowered in trees. Where the road to this cool retreat branched off, Lieutenant Duncan ordered a halt, and then, with his usual kindness, asked us to decide whether we would go to the plantation and rest till evening, or push on and finish our day's work before we halted. There was some little difference of opinion. Certain thirsty individuals, who kept up a constant sucking at their canteens, declared that they were nearly choked, notwithstanding the three pints of water each had swallowed; others, who had drunk nothing since we started, were in favor of pushing on. It ended in the lieutenant sending one of his men, laden with canteens, to the plantation, and in our resuming the march.

The Texan put his "pony" on the easy amble, which is the leading trait of a Southern horse, and struck off in a straight line toward the distant house. We could see the horse and rider gradually sinking in the prairie as they receded from us, until not much could be discerned beside the wide-brimmed Texan hat. There was a little interval, and then horse and rider re-appeared, striking off at an angle which would intercept our line of march, and travelling on the same easy amble. The horses of the Texans, I must confess, had greatly disappointed me. Half of them were miserable, ill-shaped ponies, which could never have made or withstood a charge, and were unworthy of the name of cavalry horses. And yet these mounted troops of the Confederates have shown a wonderful readiness and swiftness of movement, which have often outwitted our generals and eluded our strategy, and that too, in a country where our horses would have starved. This great "mobility" I ascribe, in part, to the ambling gait (forbidden in our service) which carries them along some five miles an hour, without strain to the horse or fatigue to the rider; and, in part, to the free use of the lariat, which enables the horse to graze at every momentary halt. Man and horse understood this latter principle, for the former never dismounted without twitching off the bridle, and the latter never stopped without industriously picking up his living. In one respect the Texans are careless of their horses, tearing off the saddles the moment they halt, and never dreaming of cold water either as a preventive or a cure of the sore back that tortures nearly every horse.

While I was making these reflections, our column had stretched out in its usual manner, and then broken into small groups: these separated more and more as we advanced. The guards told us that Turtle-Tail Bayou was to be our camping ground, and they pointed to the timber, which looked like a low cloud along the horizon. How long this cloud was in changing into trees, and how slowly these trees rose in view, no one can imagine who has not travelled *afoot* upon the prairies. The sun sent down his usual burning rays as he approached the meridian, and a damp stifling heat rose from the grass. Yet it is a great thing to be first in camp, and able thereby to choose your own tree, and label it "TAKEN," by pitching your haversack at its foot, and to lie down and rest ere the slow walkers arrive. So the two or three of us who led pushed on. The trees came slowly more and more into view; the branches imperceptibly rose; the grass beneath them appeared. Then the corporal and his men left us and rode on to select the camping ground. We followed slowlier on their trail, keeping our eyes upon them until we saw them dismount where timber and prairie met—unsaddle and turn loose their horses, the welcome signs of our coming rest. The sight gave vigor to our halting feet—on, on, without a stop, though it was two miles, as the bird flies, to the nearest tree. On, on, until panting and streaming, I tear off my hat and haversack and drop them, with myself, at the foot of a spreading oak.

There is no rest like that which comes after such exercise. I see again the little groups drawing nearer across the prairie; coming in with sun-tinted faces and dripping brows; speaking no words, unless a few tired monosyllables; casting quick glances round for some smooth, shaded spot of turf, then walking there and dropping down. And last of all, the heavy, lumbering wagon rumbling up; its tired passengers jolted, and jaded, and cross, and broiled, yet still willing to find, with particular care, a spot that pleases them, whilst the teamster pulls the clattering harness from the mules, turns them loose upon the prairie, and, like the others, sinks down to silence and repose.

Hour upon hour thus passed, partly in sleep and partly in a dreamy languor of delicious rest. Then came a little restlessness and glances at the sun—then the blue smoke of a fresh-kindled camp-fire, and assertions that A. and B. had risen, and were preparing (for themselves) the one important meal. When such assertions had been repeated twice or thrice around me, the ground, which at first was softer than down, began to grow hard, and withal somewhat knobby. I arose, and went with Lieutenant Sherman to find the bayou. It was a stagnant bed of polywogs, not ten feet wide nor ten inches deep. Crawling out on a log, nevertheless, and skimming off the green, slimy scum, we dipped up the water and enjoyed, as we had seldom enjoyed before, the luxury of a bath. Returning to the camp-fire, we found that the guards, mindful of their prisoners' more tired condition, were baking "dodgers" for all hands, and that the "dodgers" were nearly done.

One of us quickly clambered into the wagon, and cut from the side of bacon a couple of slices, while the other sharpened two slender sticks. The bacon, skewered on these, was speedily toasted over the fire. A slice of "dodger" took the place of plates and dishes; our pocket-knives were also spoons and forks; and yet this Texan supper in the open air, cooked by oneself, and eaten after a twenty mile march and a twelve hour fast, is as delicious a meal as was ever served. The blankets were spread ere the dew fell. We lay gazing on the stars, smoked lazily, and talked of to-morrow's march, till it grew dark. To me this camp brought back all the interest of an old cavalry bivouac with some of its most unpleasant parts left out. The sense of responsibility was now gone. I had no anxiety or duty beyond that of taking care of myself. There were no guards for me to post; no pickets to visit; no rounds to make, and no prisoners to watch.

Again the blankets were rolled—the bacon toasted—the dodger divided, and a cup of tea made. Of tired nature's sweet restorer, English breakfast tea—so much perverted and abused in civilized life—we had a little canister, and wondrous were the works which that little canister performed. Its few ounces of simple-looking herb—so light—so portable—so bulkless, seemed to contain strength sufficient for an army. Those who sipped it, though weary and faint, grew strong and cheerful: those who disliked it at home, confessed that it tasted like nectar on the march. Ere the last sip was taken, the corporal mounted the wagon and said, "Now, gentlemen, please to pack along your little tricks." The "little tricks" were safely stowed by the gallant corporal, on top of the rations; the sick and lame were stowed on top of them; Mrs. Stratford took the seat reserved for her; the well "fell in," and again we started.

The road crossed the timber-belt, and emerged on a lake-like prairie. It was that hour when the soft light of the morning heightened the peculiar beauty which this march revealed. The rising sun gilded the tree-tops beside us, and tinged the soft expanse before. The herds were moving slowly; some so near that we could hear the sullen bellow of the bulls; and some so distant that we could see only their long horns moving above the green, looking like wild fowl floating on the surface of the grassy sea. The prairie rose and fell in occasional swells, the distant timber swept around it in the graceful windings of a serpentine shore, and islets of trees waved upon the bosom of this green and wood-bound lake.

Before the morning passed, I had an illustration of a folly which pervades our army. The guards had warned us that it was sixteen miles across this prairie, and until it should be crossed, we should find no water. Every canteen was therefore filled, as was a two-gallon keg that had followed me through the lines. Several years ago, Lieutenant-Colonel Frederick Townsend, of the Eighteenth United States Infantry, in recounting to me his sufferings while crossing the Gila desert, had laid great stress upon the fact, that during the journey he had made it a rule to go without drinking till he halted for the night. Remembering this when I entered the army, I subjected myself to like discipline, drinking only when I ate. A single week made this a habit, and left me comparatively comfortable and independent. On this morning, I accordingly loaned my canteen to some one foolish enough to need it, and walked along without the slightest feeling of thirst. It was not eleven o'clock, and we had not marched six hours, when we came to a puddle of water, filling the wagon-track. The water was apparently the result of some local shower; it was clear, but the road was dirty, and on one side, lying in the water, were the putrid remains of an ox. I was turning out to go around the puddle, when I heard my friends behind shout to me to stop.

"What for?" I asked, in much amazement at the idea of halting in the wettest spot we could find.

"Why, for a drink."

"A drink! What, drink that filthy water?"

Yes, they were thirsty enough to drink anything. They must drink something; the canteens and keg had been empty two hours. With accelerated speed, they hurried to the margin of the puddle. Some knelt down and drank, others ladled it up in their mugs, and several actually filled their canteens with the decoction. Thus had the little period of six hours swept away the niceties of men who, in their own homes, would have sickened at the thought of this loathsome draught; and thus did a childish habit destroy the whole pleasure of their walk, hide all the beauties of the landscape, divert their attention from objects of interest, and subject them to a needless annoyance, sometimes little less than torture.

The following day passed much like the others—our road still leading us across several wood-encircled prairies, separated from each other by narrow timber-belts and trivial, dried-up bayous. Early in the afternoon, after a march of twenty-three miles, we reached a bayou possessed of two or three names. From these, I selected as the one easiest to be remembered, "Indian," and after crossing the place where the water of Indian Bayou ought to have been, I found that we were to encamp beyond the "timber," and in a little grove. This word "grove" is in constant use through western Louisiana and Texas, and when first heard, it strikes the educated ear as a specimen of the fine talk so common in all parts of our country. But when these natural *groves* are seen, the purest taste acknowledges that the word is not misapplied. The one in which we now encamped was an oval clump of the live-oak, so clear and clean below, so exact and regular in form, that one could hardly believe nature had not been aided by the gardener's art.

The next morning our breakfast disclosed the fact, that the Confederate bacon ration is not so large as the military appetite. The lieutenant informed me that he had no intention of starving in the midst of plenty, and had sent forward two men to shoot a yearling, near a certain bayou, and there we would halt and "barbecue" the meat. From the time of leaving the Teche, the prairies had been steadily growing drier. The atmosphere, too, was clearer, the sky brighter, the air more bracing and elastic, and though the sun was intensely hot, yet there was not the damp, vaporous heat that is so oppressive in the lower prairies of Louisiana. This day we were to cross a "dry-prairie," and as we had at last succeeded in an early start (4–45), we reached it before the heat of the day had begun. A very dreary waste it was, unenlivened by the usual herds, its scanty herbage dried and withered up, and its wide expanse barren and desolate. It was, if I remember aright, nine miles across, but seemed much farther, for the road was soft and sandy, and with every breeze, a cloud of dust travelled down upon us. As the nine miles lessened into one, and the stunted trees that bordered the dry-prairie came in view, our two beef-hunters also could be seen driving down their half-wild game toward the road. Being somewhat in advance, I struck off to join them. Ere I accomplished this, a young heifer broke from the herd and bounded away. Instantly one of the rifles flashed and the heifer fell. The shot attracted the corporal, and in a moment his little bay was coming pell-mell across the broken ground, leaping some gullies and scrambling in and out of others, until he threw himself back on his haunches beside us. The corporal looked with great interest at what they called the "yuhlin," inquired how far they had driven it (some eight miles), and enlarged on our great luck in getting so fat a "beef" on so poor a "range."

It was somewhat of a mystery to me how the "yuhlin" would be carried to camp. When I asked whether the wagon, or perhaps the leading pair of mules, would be brought round to tow it in, the corporal laughed, and said in his merry way, that he would show us how they carried their game home in Texas. Forthwith he took his ever-useful lariat, and making fast one end to the "yuhlin's" horns, wound the other round the horn of his Mexican saddle. One of the men attached another in like manner, and thus harnessed, the two horses dragged the heifer as they would a log. The saddles, girthed for "roping" cattle, did not yield, and the horses tugged away with as much unconcern as though they were pulling by the ordinary collar and traces.

The mile between us and the halting-place was soon passed over, and all hands seemed to feel a deep, immediate interest in the "yuhlin." Although we had marched eighteen miles that morning, it was not eleven o'clock; nevertheless there were suggestions of *fresh* steaks, and the deserter (who really seemed to try to eat all he could, so as to be in some measure even with men who had less ripened chances of being shot) proceeded to bake a dodger. The corporal had unsaddled his horse in a trice, and was now elbow deep in breaking up the "yuhlin." Another corporal—a quiet, hard-working, unassuming German—prepared the frame for barbecuing the meat. This consisted of poles placed horizontally, about three feet from the ground. Beneath it a slow fire was made, and the meat, cut up in thin slices, was spread on the poles. In three or four hours it was partly dried and partly cooked into a half-hard state, and was then said to be barbecued. Meanwhile an army of hogs came out of the woods, lean and savage, and grunted impatiently for their share of the "yuhlin." A smaller but not less impatient party waited, with drawn knives and sharpened sticks, till the steaks could be cut, and then hurried with them to their several fires. A steak thus cooked upon hard-wood embers retains a flavor that the best French *chef*, with charcoal range, only approaches. And when this flavor is intensified by the fresh breezes of the prairie, and the long miles of a day's march, it is not wonderful that men affirm that steaks cut from buffalo or stag, or even from a poor little half-tamed "yuhlin," are better than the best butcher's meat that can be bought at home.

When the meat was all barbecued, we pushed forward for the Calcasieu. The river formed a dividing line between a forest and a prairie country. At the foot of a slight bluff was a flat-boat and rope-ferry. I learnt from the ferryman, with much surprise, that our "gun-boat boats" had been up there, and captured a steamer and several schooners. I wished most ardently as we stepped aboard the flat, that they might re-appear at that particular moment, and enable us to return the good treatment of our guards, by providing for their wants in New Orleans. The wish was not realized, and the scow, like a gentler craft, wafted us to the other shore. There an unexpected individual hailed our approach, in the person of a bright-looking mule, who, solitary and sad, was travelling briskly toward the ferry. The corporal, who, as usual, led, answered the mule in his way, and quickly uncoiled the lariat. The mule tried a dodge, but the lariat flew straight over his head and tight around his neck. The mule was fairly "roped." The corporal gave an inspiriting yell, and examined the brand. It was an unknown brand—a Louisianian brand—and the mule was therefore adjudged a lawful prize.

Our road now wound through the green woods and along the bank of the winding river. The sun, which at first was behind us, moved round upon our left, then swung in front, then passed beside us on our right, then speedily changed back, and shone again before us. The foliage screened the river, but frequent openings uncovered views of these river-bends, and of the clear, dark water flowing beside us. Could a section of the Calcasieu be cut out and transplanted to the environs of some great city, the rich luxuriance of its banks, clad with verdure from the vines that trail upon the water to the tops of the tall firs and deep-green magnolias that overhang the stream—its constant windings and its graceful curves, would be deemed a marvel of picturesque beauty. Yet here the traveller finds in it only a dull monotony of never-ceasing turnings, and sees in the beautiful foliage of its banks, only a dreary loneliness. I listened to a Texan's description, and doubted whether it had ever received an admiring glance before my own. This wood, too, through which we marched, was not the foul swamp of eastern Louisiana. There was the cool, deep shade, the dreamy stillness, the sweet, wild perfume of our northern forests. The trees aided, too, in the brief delusion. We knew the rough branches of the oak and the needles of the "fadeless pine." Large gum-trees deceived us into the belief that they were the maples of a "sugar-bush;" and dwarfed magnolias, at the first glance, took the semblance of the hickory. There was also a delightful refreshingness in the cool, shadeful river-bank, and our long march through prairies, exposed and shelterless, helped us to realize "the sweet retirement" of the woods.

For four miles we marched with spirit and pleasure, although they made up the sum of twenty-five for that day's work. Then halting, on a sandy bluff covered with pines, we encountered a legion of troubles. The gnats were terrible—the mosquitoes fearful—the pine smoke spoilt our steaks—the fresh breeze of the prairie did not reach us—and our longest march was followed by a restless night. All the next day our road continued in the "piny-woods." There were occasional openings, and the ground was clear of underbrush, yet most of the party wished themselves back on the prairie, and thought the light shade of the pines a poor return for the prairie breeze. As it was Sunday, we halted early, and the lieutenant told us that one day more would bring us to Niblett's Bluff.

For two days we lay idle at the Bluff, with no better recreation than yawning and cooking. On the third, the Beaumont boat arrived. Some Vicksburg paroled prisoners had, meanwhile, come in, and they spoke of our soldiers in terms which were most cheering to us. They were as brave as men could be—they had treated them like brothers—they had given them all the rations they could carry with them, and they had behaved "a heap better every way" than it was supposed Yankees could. They said this not only to us, but to other soldiers and citizens, and spoke up boldly on our behalf. The effect was agreeable, not in any material change, but in good feeling and in the greater kindliness with which we were treated. The boat started the next morning at daybreak. We descended the Sabine and ascended the Neches, reaching Beaumont in the evening. At this place there was a railway eating-house, that gave us a greasy breakfast, for a dollar and a half; we also bought sugar for a dollar a pound, and watermelons for a dollar apiece. These prices seemed enormous at the time, but subsequent experience makes them appear quite reasonable.

We left the little town of Beaumont on an open platform car of the Houston train. Lieutenant Duncan made an effort to have us placed in the passenger cars, but they were full. The news of Vicksburg had reached here some time before us, and the coming of the Vicksburg prisoners was expected. At every station were anxious faces, sometimes made glad and sometimes going away more anxious than they came. At one of these, there were two women, evidently a mother and her daughter. The train had hardly stopped, when I heard a shriek, which sounded like one of agony, but was instantly followed by the words, "O my son, I'm so glad, I'm so glad, I'm so glad!" I looked and saw a fine young fellow, who had told us many tales of the sufferings of the siege, running toward the woman, and the next moment folded in her arms. Unconscious of the many eyes upon them, the mother hung upon his neck, and the sister held his hand. Some friends tossed him his roll of blankets, but it fell unnoticed. The train started, but they did not look around, and when we were far out upon the prairie, they still stood there exchanging their eager words, and seemingly unconscious that we had left them.

It was twilight when the train ran into Houston. A crowd was on the platform, made up of families and friends, who had come there to welcome their sons and brothers from the dreadful siege. There was a row of young girls upon the edge of the platform, and as our car was the first of the train, they of course saw us while looking for their friends. It was interesting to observe the different expressions that passed over the line of pretty faces as their eyes scanned us. At first a look of anxious interest—a shade of disappointment—a start of surprise—a slight shrinking back with side glances at each other and the whispered-word, "*prisoners*"—and then, in most cases, a little glance of pity. But our car ran past them, and the next moment were heard the usual sounds that welcome long-absent soldiers to their homes—loud congratulations, eager inquiries, laughter and kisses. A little shade of sorrow, and perhaps of envy, fell on us. We stood apart, a small group unnoticed, as unknown. I tried to repress the dangerous feeling, but insensibly my thoughts flew far away to those who would thus have welcomed us.

The kindness of Lieutenant Duncan continued unabated. We had shouldered our knapsacks, but he sent for carts, and insisted on conveying them for us. Before the Provost Marshal's, a small crowd assembled, but it was quiet and respectful. An officer of the provost guard came out. He took the roll and called it, made sure that all were present, and informed Lieutenant Duncan that he was relieved from the further charge of us. We were faced, and marched to what had been the Court House. Our old guard accompanied us. They attempted to carry in our things, but were stopped at the door. There they shook hands warmly, and wished us a speedy exchange. We turned down a dark stone passage and entered a room. There were bars on the window, and the moonlight fell in little checkered squares upon the dirty floor. The corporal of the guard brought in our baggage—sent out and bought us some bread—asked if we wanted anything else—and then drew out a key. With the sight of that key, all conversation ceased. It was a wand of silence. No one spoke or moved or looked elsewhere. Every eye remained fixed on the key. The corporal inserted it in the door. It went in slowly and grated horribly, unlike the grating of a house key, or an office key, or a safe key, or a stable key, or any kind of a key, SAVE ONE! The corporal looked around and said, good night. No one had breath enough to respond. The corporal stepped out and the door closed, not with a bang or a slam or a crash, but with a heavy, ominous, awful sound. There was still an instant of suspense, a small infinitesimal fraction of a faint hope, and then the key turned, grating with an indescribable sound, such as none of us ever heard key give forth before. With a great effort I withdrew my eyes from the door-lock, and looked around the room. All were seated on their blankets, and ranged round, with their backs against the walls. The moonlight checkers still fell on the floor. I felt that somebody must speak, that if somebody did not speak soon, some of us would never speak again. I thought that I would speak—I made another great effort, and said:

"What a singular sound a key makes when somebody else turns it; did you ever remark it before? I suppose *you* have."

One man laughed—all laughed. Lieutenant Sherman came promptly to my aid, and said:

"How pretty that moonlight is on the floor! *Who* cares for the bars."

And then we had (apparently) a very jolly evening, in the dark.

As this military prison has not a very good name among prisoners, and some who have been confined there have had to wait a day or two for rations, and then a day or two more to get them cooked, I feel bound to say that the guard brought us a very good breakfast the next morning, which I took to be a part of their own. They brought us also word that we should be sent by the morning cars to Camp Groce.

With alacrity we shouldered our knapsacks, and lugged our remaining "traps" to the cars; and with a sense akin to freedom, we hurried away from those picturesque bars and that detestable lock. There was a little detention at the depot, and then we were placed in a "first-class passenger car" with first-class passengers, and rolled along toward the prisoners' camp. The conductor soon came upon his rounds, and as he passed me, asked in a whisper, if there were any Massachusetts officers among the prisoners. He was a tall, fine-looking man, with the tightness and trimness of dress that no one ever finds in a Southerner. I asked who he was, and learnt that he was Lieutenant-Governor B——, of Massachusetts. The fact was even so—an ex-Lieutenant-Governor of Massachusetts was a conductor on the South Western Railroad of Texas!

"Here is your stopping-place, gentlemen," said the sergeant of our guard. We looked from the car windows, and saw long barracks of rough boards, like an enclosed cow-shed. In front was a pretty grove, and in the rear a sloping hill. At the doors of the barracks we saw clusters of blue-jackets, and a few sauntered around the buildings. We toiled up a sandy bank; the roll was called, and we were "turned over" to the commanding officer. Captain Buster greeted us kindly, and said he was sorry to see us; he had been a prisoner twenty-two months in the dungeons of Mexico, and knew what it was. He marshalled us down to the barracks, and formally presented us to Captain Dillingham, the senior officer of the naval prisoners. We entered the barracks. They were like most such buildings, long and narrow, with bunks around the sides, and tables for the well and cots for the sick. The officers occupied the first compartment. They crowded around us, with eager questions, and showed us kindness and hospitality beyond our expectations. We selected such bunks as were still empty, unpacked our knapsacks, and made our arrangements for the night, and the many nights that were to follow. We studied the faces of our new companions, and found that they were for the most part sick and sad. We talked to them, and found that they were unhappy and dejected. Half a year's imprisonment had manifestly changed them from energetic, active men, to listless, idle, irritable invalids. We asked ourselves whether it could have a like effect on us, and answered that it could not.

VI.

CAMP GROCE.

It is not a pleasant thing to be a prisoner; I never enjoyed it, and never made the acquaintance of any prisoner who said that he did. True is it that you have but few cares and responsibilities. In the prisoners' camp you take no heed of what you shall eat, or what you shall drink, or wherewith you shall be clothed. If the rations come, you can eat them; and if they do not, you can go without; in neither case have your efforts any thing to do with the matter. Your raiment need not trouble you; for there vanity has no place, and rags are quite as honorable as any other style of dress. You are never dunned by importunate creditors, and if, by possibility, you were, it would be a sufficient bar in law and equity to say that you would not pay. There you are not harassed by pressing engagements, or worried by clients or customers. There you have no fear of failure, and may laugh at bankruptcy. And yet, with all these advantages, no man ever seeks to stay in this unresponsible paradise.

> "The dews of blessing heaviest fall
> Where care falls too."

I found that there was a horrible sense of being a prisoner—of being in somebody's possession—of eating, drinking, sleeping, moving, living, by somebody's permission; and worst of all, *that* somebody the very enemy you had been striving to overcome. There was a feeling of dependence on those who were the very last persons on whom you were willing to be dependent. There was a dreary sense of constraint in your freest hours, of being shut in from all the world, and having all the world shut out from you.

In the first days of imprisonment the novelty carried the new prisoners along, and buoyed them up. Then came a season of work, when they built cabins and made stools and tables; and then, a restless fit, when they felt most keenly the irksomeness of the life, and made foolish plans to escape, which (so the "old prisoners" said) had been tried before and failed. Then the "new prisoners" would grow quiet and sad. The most of them would become idle, inert, neglectful of their dress and quarters, peevish and listless, despondent of exchange, yet indifferent to all present improvement. A few (about one in ten) would struggle to make matters better; they would take hopeful views of affairs and perform active work on things around them.

For a day or two after our arrival at Camp Groce we lay by, idle and weary. As I thus looked on, and saw the listless despondency of the "old prisoners," I discovered quickly that those were happiest who were busiest. Experience since has confirmed me in the value

I early set on *occupation*. Those labors which the rebels have imposed on our men—the chopping of wood—the building of houses—the cooking of rations—have been, I think, the prisoner's greatest blessings. Our active rthern minds chafe at enforced idleness, and the freshly caught Yankee, or Hoosier, after the work of cabin building is done, and the rough tables and stools are made, becomes dejected and then sick; and yet while he was doing the work at which he growled, both soul and body bore up easily. It is no wonder then that I said to my lieutenant, "This will never do for us, Sherman, we *must* be busy."

We turned over a new leaf, therefore, for the following day. The Captain of the "Morning Light" joined us and pledged himself to provide and devise quantities of work. With the first gleam of light one of us rose, and from a little private hoard abstracted a small handful of coffee. These sailor prisoners, I early found, had no idea of going without while the Confederacy could supply them for either love or money (they did not care much which); and they inspired the rest with a little of their own easy impudence.

Accordingly on the door-post hung one of the last coffee-mills that the shops of Houston had held, and in the galley (as they called the kitchen) stood a stove—the only one, probably, in any Texan camp. The first riser then kindled a fire in the stove, if it was not already there, and ground and made the coffee. Then bearing it to the sleepers' bunks, he quickly roused them with the cheerful salutation of "Here's your coffee—your fine hot coffee!" When a tin mug of coffee is the only luxury of the day it rises in importance and becomes great. We sipped it slowly and discussed it gravely. One thought that if it were strained a fourth time it would be stronger—the maker, on the contrary, thought that straining it again would take the strength out; a second insisted that it ought to boil—but the maker maintained that boiling dispelled the aroma and sent it flying through the air. The coffee ended before the argument; and then after rinsing out our mugs and restoring them to their private pegs, we took down our towels and started for the "branch." We descended the hill by a little path that was nearly hidden in tall weeds and led to some thick bushes and trees that grew along the "branch." The chain of sentinels around the camp consisted of broad-hatted Texans, sitting at irregular intervals on stumps and logs, and generally engaged in balancing their rifles on their knees. One of these, Captain Dillingham hailed in a patronizing way, in return for which attention the sentry halted us.

"I reckon," he said, "you can't go no further jist yit awhile."

"Halloo," said the Captain, "what's the matter now?"

"Well, there be three down there now, and the orders is not to let no more down to once."

"Orders?" said the Captain, indignantly: "who cares for orders! What difference does it make to Jeff Davis whether there are three prisoners or six washing themselves?"

"Well, I reckon it don't make an awful sight of difference," the sentry admitted.

"Of course it doesn't," said the Captain, following up the concession. "The idea of making us wait *here* because there's somebody down *there!*"

"Well, I reckon you might as well go on," yielded the sentry: "I reckon you won't run off this morning;" and on we went.

The "branch" was a little brook, sometimes running over sand-bars, sometimes filtering through them, and occasionally settling into pools, which were our bathing places. It was a happy relief to be out of sight of the barracks and alone. We clung to this under all sorts of difficulties and restrictions—sometimes going out with a patrol—sometimes squeezing through on parole, and holding fast to it, until we left Camp Groce in the cold weather of December.

The bath being taken, we walked leisurely back, wondering that so few sought this relief from the misery of prison. At the barracks our sailor cook had prepared the breakfast, which was set out on the long table. He blew his boatswain's whistle, and all members of the mess hurried at the call. I had felt poor when I arrived at Camp Groce. I had expected to broil beef on sticks, and bake dodger in a dodger pot, and live on my ration as the Texans did. I was amazed at the extravagance I beheld, and when Captain Dillingham, with a sailor's heartiness, invited me to join the navy mess, I hinted to him that probably I should become insolvent in a fortnight, if I did. The Captain laughed at the idea. He said there was plenty of money in Texas—he had never seen a country that had so much money—and it was the easiest thing to get it—anybody would lend you all you wanted—the only fault he had to find was, that after he got it he couldn't spend it. Now, making reasonable allowances for nautical exaggeration, this was true. Sometimes a secret Unionist—sometimes a Confederate officer fairly forced his money upon us. They took no obligation, save the implied one of our honor; and the manner of payment, and the specie value of their Confederate funds, they left entirely to ourselves. To spend this money was a harder task. To change this easily gotten spoilt paper into something of real intrinsic worth was to acquire wealth.

When breakfast was finished, I took up a little French volume of ghost stories (which I read over five times carefully in the course of the next five months), and spent on it and some military works the next four hours. "Prisoners have nothing to do but to eat;" so at the end of four hours we had our breakfast over again. When "dinner," as it was called, was finished, the Captain stoutly asserted that a load of wood must be got, and somebody must volunteer to get it. The Captain volunteered, so did Lieutenant Sherman and myself, so did another officer cheerfully, and two more tardily; but the mass of closely confined prisoners were too weak and too dejected, and they shrunk back from the effort that this work would cost them, preferring to stay idle and listless in their horrid prison. Those of us who volunteered, seized a couple of dull old axes, and proceeded to head-quarters.

"We are going out for wood to cook with," said the Captain to the lieutenant that we found there, "and we must have an arbor to keep the sun off those sick fellows, or they'll all die, and you'll have nobody to exchange. Wake up one or two of your men, and send them out with us."

The lieutenant reckoned he could not, he hadn't a man to spare, all were on guard who hadn't gone off to a race. The Captain pointed to the axes and said, "we were all ready to go." This struck the lieutenant as a powerful reason, and he reckoned he would let a nigger hitch up the mules, and then let us go without any guard, but we must not go across the "branch." The Captain replied that we would not go a great way across the "branch;" but he was fond of liberty, he said, and would not be circumscribed by "branches." The lieutenant insisted on the "branch," there had been orders given to that effect, he reckoned. The Captain did not care anything about orders—what difference could it make to Jeff. Davis, he asked, whether we cut wood on this side of the "branch" or the other. The lieutenant could not answer this question, so he said, coaxingly, "Well, you won't go a great ways on the other side, will you?"

This little difference being thus compromised, we mounted an old rickety "two-mule wagon," and drove down the "wood road," till a sentry, sitting on a stump, reckoned we had better stop. *Stop!* what should we stop for? He reckoned he'd orders to let nobody out. *Orders!* Why, we had just been up to headquarters, and got orders to go out, and also the wagon; what more could he want. Then why had not the lieutenant sent down a man to tell him; it was no way to do business. The Captain said the wagon was pass enough as long as the mules would travel, and that we were going out for wood, which he thought altered the case; if he, the sentry, doubted it, there were the axes. The sentry looked at the axes, and could not doubt the evidence of his eyes, so he let us out.

The sun went down, and then began a long evening. There was nothing to do but to sit in the dark and talk of nothing. Then there was a detail made of two for the sick watch, and finding that I was "on," I went to bed. In the morning there had been several late sleepers who wondered why people got up early and ran a coffee-mill. As a matter of course these individuals now wondered why people went to bed early and wanted to sleep. The topics, too, which they chose were exactly the topics that always keep you awake; and if by chance you forgot them long enough to fall asleep, then there would be a furious argument on some important matter; and if that did not waken you, then some other man (who, like yourself, turned in at taps,) would lose patience and roar out, "taps," "lights out," "guard-house," etc., etc.

In small assemblages men may wake up and fall asleep when they please, but in camps and barracks, where many men of different habits are brought together, there must be some uniform rule for all. The Confederates never enforced military usage upon us, much to the regret of all who were accustomed to it, and a few very early and very late individuals, some of whom sat up till after taps, and others of whom turned out before reveille, were an endless annoyance to each other and to all. I think no officer of experience ever ran this gauntlet without inwardly resolving that, if ever he got back to his own command, stillness and darkness should rule between taps and reveille; that with daylight every blanket should go out, and every tent be put in order; that every shaggy head should be clipped, and all the little regulations which weak-minded recruits think to be "military tyranny," should be most rigorously enforced.

But as I tossed around and made these resolves, the little sailor who was acting as hospital steward came in with both hands full of prescriptions. We had two excellent and faithful surgeons at Camp Groce, Dr. Sherfy of the "Morning Light," and Dr. Roberts of the Confederate service. They kept their little office outside of the lines, came round on their second visit in the afternoon, and during the evening made up their prescriptions. This evening the first watch took the prescriptions from the hospital steward, and received the directions. It was Lieut. Hays, of the 175th N. Y., a happy, generous, warm-hearted Irishman, youthful and with the humor and drollery of his race. He was always making fun when others were dull, and making peace when they were angry. Soon I heard him going round among the sick. "I will listen," I thought, "and find out what I have to do when my watch comes."

"Here's your medicine now, Mr. Black," I heard him say, "wake up and take it."

"What is it?" asked the sick man.

"Oh! it's blue pills to touch your liver; come, take it, and don't be asking questions."

"How many of them are there?" inquired the patient after swallowing several.

"There are just seven of them, but what's that to you? it won't do you any good to know it."

"Why, the doctor said he would send me six. Perhaps you are not giving me mine."

"Just you take what's sent to you. If you don't take the whole seven, they won't touch your liver a bit; six would be of no use at all."

The man with the untouched liver swallowed the pills, and soon I heard the first watch rousing another sick man with the same formula of "Here's your medicine now, wake up and take it—it's blue pills to touch your liver."

"How many of them are there?" asked this patient.

"There are just six of them—what's the use of your knowing?"

"Why, the doctor said he would send me seven—perhaps these are not mine."

"No matter, six are just as good as seven, and seven are just as good as fifty. All you need do is to take what I give you, and it will touch your liver all the same."

Much enlightened by this mode of distributing doses, and re-assuring patients, I went to sleep, and slept till one A.M., when the first watch called me, and I took my turn. It was rather dreary, sitting in the dark and cold, occasionally giving a man his medicine or a drink, and wishing for daylight. There was one poor fellow, also a lieutenant of the 175th, fast going in consumption. His constant cough, his restless sleep, his attenuated form, bright eye and hectic cheek, all told of the coming end. Yet with him there was nothing to be done but wait and watch.

Now this, of itself, was not such a bad sort of day; but there was a month of such days; and then another month, and then a third, and then many more. What wonder that the strongest resolutions failed!

Then death came in among our little company, and came again and again. Then sickness increased under the August sun. The long moss that hung down from the trees and waved so gracefully on the breeze, had betokened it long before it came, and the uncleaned camp and listless life made the prediction sure. It went on until all but one had felt it in some shape or other, and there were not enough well to watch the sick. It never left us, and down to our last day at Camp Groce the chief part of our company were frail and feeble and dispirited.

Near to the barracks stood a little shanty of rough boards, divided by a plank partition into two rooms. One of these had been assigned to Mr. Stratford and his wife, and the other after several weeks came into the possession of Col. Burrill of the 42d Mass., Dr. Sherfy, Capt. Dillingham and myself. After living amid the sickness, the discord, and the misery of the barracks, this room measuring ten feet by twelve, promised to four of us a quiet and retirement that amounted almost to happiness. We went to work upon our little house with all the zeal of school-boys, and positively look back upon it with affection. It boasted doors, but neither windows nor chimney. Its walls were without lath and plaster, and through innumerable chinks let in the wind. The Captain and I also messed with Mr. and Mrs. Stratford; so we had a double interest in the shanty, and when we had built ourselves bunks and swung a shelf or two, we went to work on our other half.

"What shall I do for a blanket line?" was one of the first questions I had asked after our arrival.

"Let me lend you mine," said an officer of the "Morning Light," "we sailors always hang on to our ropes."

"I will take it this morning, with thanks; but I want something of my own. If there is anything I despise, it's a soldier's blanket in his tent after reveille."

"We are not so particular here, I'm sorry to say," said my friend; "and unless you can find a line among the sailors, you won't find one in Texas."

"I am going out in the woods this afternoon, with

Mr. Fowler," I answered, "and will try to get one there."

Now, Mr. Fowler, the acting Master of the "Morning Light," was an old sailor, who had hardly been on shore for forty years. But in his early boyhood he had watched the Indians at their work, and caught from them, as boys do, some of their simple medicines and arts. For years and years these facts had slept undisturbed in his mind. If any one had asked him, he would have said they were forgotten; but now, under the pressure of our wants, they, one by one, came back. With this long-time worthless knowledge, Mr. Fowler was now busily and usefully employed. He made Indian baskets of all shapes and sizes, and even bent his ash-slips into fantastic dishes. He made Indian brooms and fly-brushes, and wooden bowls, and wove grape-vine and black-jack into high-backed, deep-seated, sick-room chairs. Where others saw only weeds or fire-wood, he found remedies for half our diseases; and when the surgeon's physic gave out, Mr. Fowler's laboratory was rich in simples.

We went out on parole that afternoon, Mr. Fowler carrying his basket, and I, an axe. He called attention to the fact that these pecan nuts would be ripe by-and-by, and that those persimmons would be worth coming after when the frost should have sugared them, and he filled his basket as he walked and talked. Before long, we saw some clean black-jack vines hanging from the top-most branches of a tree. We tugged and strained a few minutes, and then a splendid vine came down, not thicker than a lady's finger at the root, yet forty feet in length. It was flexible as a rope, and as I coiled it up, I said to Mr. Fowler, "I have got my blanket line."

Having cut an ash stick for a broom, and a pecan log for an axe handle, we went back to camp, where, soon after, Mr. Fowler was busily engaged in pounding his ash stick to loosen the splints, and I, at work on the severest manual effort of my life, viz., whittling with a soft-bladed penknife, out of flinty pecan wood, an orthodox American axe-helve.

Some weeks passed, and then one of those events occurred which are doubly mortifying if you are then on the wrong side of the enemy's lines. I was lying ill in my bunk when an excited individual rushed into the barracks and made me better by the announcement, that the train had brought up great news from Houston. Blunt was coming down through the Indian Territory with his rough borderers, and all the troops in Texas were to be hurried northward to repel the invasion. For several days and nights trains ran by our camp loaded with soldiers who howled horribly to our guards, who howled horribly back to them. The "Houston Telegraph" came filled with orders of General Magruder, directing the movement of his forces, and naming twenty-seven different battalions that were to hurry forward immediately. The General did not *publish* such orders ordinarily, and this one looked like haste, excitement and alarm.

One night, about ten o'clock, an engine was heard hurrying up the road. As usual it stopped at the water-tank near our camp. In ten minutes important news had leaped from the engine to head-quarters; from head-quarters to the guard-house, and from the guard-house straight through the line of sentries into our bunks. The news was this: twelve Yankee gun-boats, twenty-four large transports, and six thousand men lay off Sabine.

The next day the train confirmed the news. We learnt, too, that Union men, in Houston, were bold and defiant, and talked openly of a change of masters. Our guards were in a ferment. They talked with us freely, and confessed that there were not three hundred troops between Houston and Sabine. "Your folks will seize the railroad and march straight on to Houston," they said, "and then Galveston will have to go, and like as not you'll be guarding us within a week." "What splendid strategy," said everybody. "Blunt has drawn all the forces in the State up to Bonham—there is nothing to prevent our coming in below; Magruder is completely out-generalled. We must forgive the two months of idleness since Vicksburg and Port Hudson fell."

Another day came, and the excitement increased; another, and affairs seemed in suspense; a third, and there was a rumor that two gun-boats had been sunk, their crews captured, and that the "Great Expedition" was "skedaddling" (such was the ignominious term applied) back to New Orleans. There came yet another day, when we sat waiting for the train.

"The cars are late," said one. "It is past three o'clock, and they should have been here at two."

"That's a good sign," said another; "it shows they have something to keep them. When they come you will see Magruder is sending off his ordnance stores."

"Then you don't feel any fear about that rumor?"

"That rumor, oh no! It is the best sign of all. They never fail to get up such rumors when they are being beaten. Don't you remember how, just before Vicksburg surrendered, we used to hear that Breckenridge had taken Baton Rouge, and Taylor was besieging New Orleans, and Lee had burnt Philadelphia?"

"Oh no," said everybody, stoutly, "there is no danger. And how can there be? We know that there is nothing down there but a little mud fort, with fifty men in it, and six forty-two pounders. Our hundred-pound Parrots will knock it to pieces, and a couple of companies can carry it by assault. Oh no, all I am afraid of is, that *we* shall be run off, nobody knows where."

The whistle sounded and we waited for the news. The track ran through a deep cutting, which at first hid the body of the cars from our sight, but a man stood on the roof of the foremost baggage car and waved his hat. Presently a howl was given by those of our guard who were waiting at the station.

"What can that mean?" said everybody. "Very strange! surely there can be no bad news for us."

The next moment, some one exclaimed, "Good heavens, what a sight! Look there!" I looked; the train was covered with the blue-jackets of our navy.

The officers of the "Clifton" and "Sachem" did not accompany their men. We heard that they were guilty of spiking their cannon, flooding their magazines, secreting their money, and other like offences, for which they were kept at Houston; later, however, they unexpectedly came up. A new Captain, who then commanded Camp Groce, ushered them in, and we welcomed them. The youngest of us then had been prisoners more than three months, and felt ourselves to be "old-prisoners." The Captain of the "Clifton" supped with us, and as he surveyed our little shanty, replete with black-jack lines, hat-racks of curiously twisted branches, knives, and spoons, and salt-cellars, neatly carved from wood, and pipes fashioned out of incomparable corn-cob, he said that these little luxuries made him feel sorry for us, for they showed him what straits we had been reduced to. I felt sorry for him as he said it, for the speech reminded me of the lessons reserved for him to learn. Later than usual we retired, excited with this unusual event. The barracks had just grown quiet, when the Captain in command suddenly re-appeared, his guard at his back. "The gentlemen who arrived to-day," he said, in an agitated voice, "will please to rise immediately." The new-comers rose, groped round for clothes and baggage in the dark; and as they dressed, asked what all this meant. The Captain vouchsafed no reply, but in a still more agitated voice, begged them to be as quick as possible. Whether they were going to be searched, or executed, or sent back to Houston, nobody could determine. They were marched off, and we, now wide awake, discussed the matter for some hours. The next morning disclosed our friends haplessly shivering around a small building, some three hundred yards distant. It appeared that strict orders had been sent up with the prisoners, directing that they should be confined separately, and hold no communication with us. The now unhappy Captain had not thought it worth while to read his orders until bed time. Then he stumbled on the fiat of the stern Provost Marshal General, whose chief delight was to court-martial Confederate captains. Deeply dismayed, he had rushed to the guard-house for his guard, to the barracks for his prisoners, and executed the painful work of separation.

The Provost Marshal General had not enclosed subsistence in his order. In the absence of dodger-pots, the "old prisoners" had to take care of these new ones. We were not allowed to write or talk, to send messages or to receive them. The baskets, as they went and came, were searched, the dodgers broken open, and everything was done in a very military and terrible way. In a few days we received a present of pea-nuts from our friends. We were not fond of pea-nuts, and did not appreciate the gift. The basket travelled over as usual with their dinner, but carried no acknowledgment of the pea-nuts. In the afternoon Lieutenant Dane, of the signal corps, was seen approaching our lines with a prize—a prize that had neither predecessor nor successor—a leg of mutton. The lieutenant delivered the mutton across the line to one of us, and the notability of the event warranted him in saying before the guard:

"This is a present from Major Barnes. Did you get the pea-nuts we sent you this morning?"

"Yes, yes," responded Captain Dillingham, on behalf of our mess; "yes, they're very nice. We are much obliged to you."

"Eat them," said the lieutenant, "eat them. They won't hurt you—eat them all."

The Captain carried the leg of mutton in, and hurriedly took down the pea-nuts. We looked sharply at them, but saw nothing unusual. Why eat them *all?* "If they want us to do so, it must be done!" We proceeded to break the shells. Presently there was a shell—a sound and healthy shell—within which had grown a long, narrow slip of paper, rolled up tightly. It contained a single message, viz., that the covered handle of Mr. Fowler's basket was in fact a mail-bag. From that time on, the watchful patrols would lift out the plates, and inspect the beef, and scrutinize the dodger, and then carry the mail-bag backward and forward for us.

With the increased number of prisoners, there had been a change in the command of the camp. The company of volunteers were relieved by a battalion of militia. To our surprise, the militia very far surpassed the volunteers, and did their business in a very soldierly way. The battalion was commanded by Lieutenant-Colonel John Sayles, a lawyer of considerable distinction in Texas. The Lieutenant-Colonel was a man of few words, very quiet, very kind, and rarely gave an order that did not effect an improvement.

On the Sunday after he assumed command, Colonel Sayles informed me in his quiet way, that there would be Divine service in the grove, and invited me and all the prisoners to accompany him. There had been a reverend gentleman preaching at Camp Groce the Sunday before I arrived, who had been seeking a chaplaincy, and had assumed what he supposed was a popular train of argument; as for instance, warning his beloved brethren that the chief horror of eternal punishment would be meeting the President of the United States there. I do not care to hear irreverent things said in the pulpit, nor do I think it the part of an officer to listen voluntarily to denunciations of his government, yet I felt assured that Colonel Sayles would not invite me to anything of that kind, and I thought I could best acknowledge his civility by accepting.

When the clergyman who officiated first caught sight of the prisoners, forming one-half of his audience, he evinced a little embarrassment. He alluded to this as he began his sermon, and spoke happily of the breadth of the Christian faith, extending to all conditions of men, and enabling enemies to stand together and worship at one altar. His prayer was chiefly an affecting and beautiful petition on our behalf. He spoke of the tender ties that were severed, and besought consolation for our distant dear ones, who must be now in anxiety watching our fate. He prayed, too, that "we their captors and keepers, may have grace to treat them as becomes Christian soldiers, resisting the evil passions of our hearts and the evil counsels of wicked and cruel men."

After the services were concluded, we were introduced to the clergyman, Mr. McGown, of Huntsville. He visited us in our quarters, ministered to our sick, and was always one of our most welcome visitors. He had been with Houston in the war of Texan independence, and was one of the heroes of San Jacinto. His acquaintance with the General had been intimate, and he entertained us with many interesting anecdotes of him and tales of the former war.

These anecdotes of General Houston then possessed for us unusual interest. When some of the older prisoners had been sent to the State Prison at Huntsville, they were halted a few minutes on the outskirts of the town. As they waited there, a tall, imposing old man approached and asked, who was the United States officer highest in rank. Captain Dillingham was pointed out to him as the senior naval officer. Walking up to him and extending his hand, he said, in a deep, emphatic voice, "My name is Houston, sir. I have come to say to you, gentlemen, that I do not approve of such treatment for prisoners of war. No prisoner of war shall ever be put in a jail with my consent."

The death of General Houston occurred just before I

reached Texas. Many stories were told of his great personal power, and strange incidents of his wondrously romantic life. The forebodings of his celebrated letter were all realized before he died, for his oldest son was in the ranks—his warmest friends and supporters were scattered and slain, and ruin and desolation brooded over the State which he had established and so long directed and controlled. He was guarded in the expression of his political sentiments, but occasionally addressed the troops, speaking from the *Texan* point of view. He never took the oath of allegiance to the Confederate Government. A short time before his death travellers were required to have a Provost Marshal's pass, and to procure a pass they must take the oath. The General had neither taken the oath nor procured a pass. He set out, however, on a journey and proceeded till one of the provost guard halted him and demanded his pass.

"My pass through Texas," said the old man, in his sternest tone, "is San Jacinto."

The Texan soldier looked at him for a moment. "I reckon," he said, "*that* pass will go as far in Texas as any a Provost Marshal ever wrote. Pass on, old San Jacinto."

Colonel Sayles was soon succeeded by Major James S. Barnes of the same battalion. The Major was a Georgian by birth, an old Texan by residence, and a man of great general information, and so far as we were concerned, in every thought and word and deed a perfect Christian gentleman. He told stories with a graphic simplicity I have never heard excelled, and was so pleasantly reasonable and so enticingly good-natured that even our wayward sailors consented to be led by a landsman, and allowed that he was as good a man as a rebel could be. One day as the Major passed through the barracks chatting with the well and cheering up the sick, he hinted at the uncertainty of exchange and at coming "northers," and advised us to prepare for the worst by building ourselves chimneys and fire-places. He promised to provide an old negro chimney-builder to engineer the work and teams to haul the material. The dwellers in the shanty quickly availed themselves of the offer. But nothing could induce those in the barracks to go and do likewise. So weak and dispirited were all that the difficulties appeared insurmountable. When the frost came aud found them still prisoners, they piled sand on the floor, and making fire upon it sat there and shivered, while the smoke floated over them and found its way out through the holes in the roof.

We, who were wise betimes, cut our logs in the woods, dug up our clay on the neighboring hill-side, and waited the arrival of "Uncle George." This uncle came in time, and led the work. A hole was cut in Mr. Stratford's room—the logs were notched and crossed, the chimney splints were split and laid up, and the whole was properly cemented together, and daubed over with rich clay mortar.

Hardly was the chimney complete, when one of the guard announced that he reckoned there'd be a norther;

the beeves, he said, were making for the timber. In Texas it is an establi hed fact that nobody can tell anything about the weather, so we gave little heed to the prediction. Early in the afternoon, however, some one said that the norther was in sight. The day was warm; the sun was bright; birds were singing, and the leaves still were green. There was nothing to indicate a change save a black cloud rapidly rising in the north. Our men were sitting round in their shirt-sleeves, whittling and working as usual, and every thing continued pleasant. The black cloud, however, bore swiftly down upon us. As it drew near, we saw an immense flock of turkey-buzzards driven before it, whirling in the air and screaming wildly. A moment later the breeze struck us. It felt not unlike the gust that precedes a thunder-shower, but as I watched the cloud I found that I had suddenly grown cold. I had heard fearful stories of these northers, and read of a hardy Vermonter, who, scorning a cold that merely skimmed the ponds with ice, had ventured out in one; and how his blood congealed, and he was carried back by his horse insensible. I saw that all the men had gone in, and that the sentries had wrapped themselves in their blankets. Within the shanty I found our little fire-place bright and its owners sitting in a close circle around it. But the cold seemed to beat directly through the walls, and the wind blew a steady blast. We passed all the long evening closely crouched around the fire, warming first one side and then the other, talking of home and pitying the poor wretches in the barracks. When bed-time came we carried hot stones with us into our bunks and hurried to bed before we should be chilled. I wrapped myself in my double army blanket with which I had braved ice and snow and then rolled myself in my buffalo. I thought it sufficient for an Arctic winter, but ere morning the horrible cold crept in and penetrated to the very bones. As I moved about to try and make my blood circulate, Colonel Burrill spoke and said that he was so cold that he feared he was dying. The Colonel had been quite ill, and this startled me; so I rose, threw a coat or two upon him, and then drawing the blankets over his head, tucked them tightly in and left him to take the chances of suffocation or freezing. I went back to my own couch and shivered away till morning. The cold drove us all out early, and we met again around our fire-place. A sailor boy brought up a hot breakfast, for cooking over a hot stove that morning was a high privilege which no one threw away. He told us that one of his shipmates lay frozen in his bunk, and that they had just found him there dead. During the morning we suspended our blankets from the rafters so as to form a little tent immediately around the fire, and there in darkness we sat the live-long day. Another dismal evening followed and another bitter night. Then, after thirty-six hours of fury, the norther went down and we ventured to crawl out and resume our work.

VII.

TEA.

THERE was some coffee in Camp Groce, when we arrived—not much—and a little was bought afterward for "morning coffee," with some tea for the sick, at fifteen dollars per pound. It was poor stuff, and not worth the price.

The messes that I found there used corn; or, as they called it, corn coffee. This was made from the meal. Burnt in a frying-pan upon the stove, by a sailor-cook, some particles in charcoal and some not singed at all, it formed a grayish compound, and made as horrible a beverage as any one could be supposed willing to drink. I thought at first that I would go back, for my own part, to an old habit of cold water; and if we had possessed pure water I might have done so. But our well-water had a sulphurous taste; and then, in this southern climate, there is an insatiable appetite for nervine food. Thus those who never touched pepper, nor cared a fig for seasoning and spices at home (not because they disliked them, but because they thought it wisest not to eat what they did not want), have had a constant craving in the army for coffee, tea, and spices, and for the bad catsups, and worse imitation sauces, that sutlers sell and soldiers buy. So I drank these slops, and, like the others, called them coffee.

A little mess, indeed, as I have hinted, applied the Louisiana lesson we had learnt, and made their "morning coffee." Turning out with the first glimmer of dawn, we ground and re-ground exactly twenty of the precious berries, watchful that not one should be lost, nor a speck of the priceless dust spilt. An old tin cylinder, with a piece of flannel bound tightly round the end, formed the strainer, and a large-sized tin mug our coffee-pot; and by keeping a week's grounds, at least, in the strainer, it was wonderful what strength this ingenious apparatus did extract.

But the enterprising Yankee mind, never long contented with any thing, quarrelled with the corn-meal coffee and proposed a change. A hardy sailor, of New England origin, objected to the *meal*, and insisted that it would be better to make the coffee directly out of corn—we should, he said, get all the flavor then. There was a furious debate over this, of course, for the enterprising Yankee mind much prefers a theory to a fact. It was argued on the one side, that the flavor was just what you did not want; that corn was corn, and it made no difference if it was also meal; and that it was much wiser to use the meal and thereby make the enemy grind our coffee, than to burn the corn and grind it ourselves. These arguments were met by others equally strong, and the debate continued till some stupid person of Dutch descent, suggested that the proof of the pudding is in the eating, and that if any one wanted to try corn for coffee, he might.

We traded some of our meal ration for corn; the corn was burnt and ground and tried, and found far preferable to meal and all other substitutes. Its opponents drank it, and our little coffee-mill creaked and rattled at all hours under the load which the discovery threw upon it.

A further improvement was effected, for it was discovered one day, that the outside of the kernel would be well parched, while the inside would have a yellow, undone appearance. The fact is, it was impossible to roast it through, and this gave to the coffee a raw, mealy taste. The remedy was simple, and consisted merely in not grinding the corn, and thus using only the outside of the kernel.

We thought then that we had reached the perfection of corn, and the last of substitutes.

There was, however, a tea made by the Texans from the leaves of a half bush, half tree, called *yapon*, which was said to taste wonderfully like the real. They drank it three times a day, at Captain Buster's head-quarters, and many of the sailors followed the fashion. Yet it had a bad name. It was said, that it caused certain unpleasant medical effects, and one young gentleman, who had once taken a mug full, averred that he shortly thereafter felt a burning sensation in that part of his body where he supposed (erroneously) was his stomach.

I never could find the men whom it was said to have made sick, and I had little belief in the rumor. Yet, as I do not like tea except when ill, there was little inducement to experiment with this unknown, untried plant. Still I meant to test it, some time or other, as a matter of scientific curiosity, and if it were like the Chinese plant, to carry a handful home for the edification of tea drinkers there.

This "some time or other" did not come, probably because the material was always close at hand. The yapon grew thickly along the brook and up to the borders of the camp. It was generally from ten to twenty feet high, and as thick as a man's arm; it had furnished us with nearly all the poles for a rustic arbor, that ran along the sunny side of the barracks, and helped to shade and cool the sick-bunks. Its branches, too, had been used to fill up in roofing the arbor, and there were leaves enough there to furnish an army with bohea.

Thus time glided away under the influence of corn coffee, till one day it was said, that the commanding officer had proclaimed corn coffee unhealthy, nay, dangerous. There were then numerous medical symptoms, all pointing forward to intermittent fever and backward to corn coffee. When a dozen men compare notes, and find that they are all afflicted in the same way, and never in their lives have been so before, it alarms them.

The surgeon was informed of this, and he thought

there must be something in it, the intermittent cases had increased so unaccountably. As we thus deliberated, Colonel Sayles came up and we consulted him. The Colonel gave his facts and recommended sweet potatoes as a substitute for corn and coffee.

"Let us look at the analysis," said the surgeon, walking into his office and taking down a big book.

"'Corn or maize, sometimes called Indian corn. This grain is cultivated throughout the United States.'" "Yes, we know that." "'Its analysis shows starch, sugar, *sulphate of lime.*' That must be the agent (if any) which is doing us all the damage. I really think you had better follow the Colonel's advice and take up the sweet potatoes."

"Let us see what the potato has in it. Doctor, who knows but that there's some other atom to be roasted into poison there?"

"Batata, yes, 'batata, or common potato,' 'seed poisonous,' and so forth. Analysis sugar, and so forth. It has the sulphate again and more of it than there is in corn. That will never do, to say nothing of costing ten dollars a bushel."

October was drawing toward its end when there came a "wet norther," and with it a sharp frost, ice thick as a pane of glass—much suffering—some agues and countless colds.

The "norther" found me ill with a periodical return of my Louisiana malarial, and brought me a cold of the severest kind. It blew through the cracks and crannies of the barracks, through my blankets and through me. I felt as though my blood had ceased to circulate and I should never be warm again.

"Try some of Mr. Fowler's sumach," suggested some one; "it cured my cold."

"I have tried everything," I said, "and find the only thing is prevention—nothing cures these colds with me when they have come."

"And I never got any help from medicine," said my friend. "But this stuff of Fowler's cured mine in a night. I never knew any thing like it."

I went to Mr. Fowler and got the sumach berries. A cluster or two thrown in a quart mug of boiling water made the remedy. It was fearfully acid, and it took fearful quantities of sugar to make it palatable, but it then had quite a pleasant taste and worked (let me say for the benefit of the victims of violent catarrh) a miraculous cure.

I had not paid much attention to the Acting Master's simples, having no great faith in medicine and less in herbs—but this with the dread of another bilious attack aroused me so far that I walked round the barracks and asked after the livers of all the patients who had been treated with his wild peach bark. These livers were found to be in a highly improved condition, and thinking it fair that mine should have a share in all the medical advantages afforded by a residence in Texas, I determined to treat it also to wild peach bark.

The "norther" broke on the second day, and in the

after noon the weather was much like the last part of one of our cold nor'-easters. The rain had ceased, but the clouds floated gloomily overhead and the wind blew coldly from the north.

"Come, Stratford," I said, "I am a convert to the Fowler treatment, and shall feel the better for a little exercise. Let us go out and get some bark."

"Oh, it's too cold and the ground will be muddy; you had better wait till to-morrow; it will be fine weather then."

"No, no, to-morrow you will be at work on the chimney, and this is a broken day; let us go now."

"Well, if you will get the patrol we will go."

I walked down to the guard-house and represented to the sergeant of the guard the importance of having wild peach bark and the necessity of going out to get it.

The sergeant first raised the usual difficulties and then gave the usual order. A stout gentleman, who helped himself to a double-barrelled gun, informed us that he would go as Pat Roll. He sketched briefly his life for us by stating that he was born in South Carolina, raised in Alabama, druv stage in Florida, and sogered it in Texas. He also expressed the opinion that Texas was an easy country to live in, "because the hogs run in the woods and the horses run out," and he intimated that he looked with great contempt on those parts of the world where the hogs eat corn, and the horses live in the stable.

As I was still weak I handed my axe over to one of

the others. We crossed the brook and near by found a wild peach. It was soon cut down, and we proceeded as usual to shave off the bark from the trunk of the tree, and then pull up such roots as would come. When this was done each of my companions loaded himself with an unpealed log, while I took the axe and basket of bark. Thus laden, we started to return.

"Since we are working for the Herb Department," said I, "let us take up some yapon and try the tea. I wonder if I can cut off this branch with one hand?"

A well-leaved branch of the yapon hung over the road, bright with red berries, and against it I raised the axe. A couple of blows brought it down. Mr. Stratford added it to his load, and with it we went back to our quarters.

A day or two passed, during which the weather moderated. It was Saturday afternoon, and I was sitting in the sun, still languid, while Mr. Stratford was trying to heat red-hot an old shovel he had found, in order that he might cut off its rivets and fit in it a new handle, when the thought of the yapon came into my head. I took up the branch and began to pluck off the leaves.

"Are you going to try the yapon?" said Lieutenant Sherman, who casually came in.

"Yes, and I want you to go up to the galley and dry the leaves?"

"Oh, why don't you take them green? That's the way the sailors do."

"True! but the sailors are not remarkable for skill in

scientific cookery, and I think a decoction of any green plant must differ a good deal from that of a dry one."

"Then why don't you take some of the leaves from the arbor?"

"They are all bleached and washed to pieces. A horse would not eat hay that had been hung up in the rain and dew as they have. Go into the doctor's office and get his Dispensatory, and we will prepare them as the Chinese do. The book must give the process for tea, for I was looking at 'sweet potatoes' the other day, and found accidentally that it is very full on the making of sugar."

The lieutenant brought the book, turned to the article, and read:

"'TEA.—The plant which furnishes tea. *Thea Chinensis* is an evergreen shrub, belonging to'"——

"Never mind the botany, we do not mean to grow tea, but cure it. Go over to the manufacture."

He skipped over a page or two and proceeded:

"'It is propagated from the seeds. In three years the plant yields leaves for collection, and in six attains the height of a man. When from seven to ten years old, it is cut down, in order that the numerous shoots which issue from the stumps may afford a large product of leaves. These are picked separately by the hand. Three harvests, according to Koempfer, are made during the year. As the youngest leaves are the best, the product of the first collection is most valuable, while that of the third, consisting of the oldest leaves, is comparatively little esteemed. After having been gathered, the leaves are dried by artificial heat in a shallow iron pan.' "

"That's a shovel," said Mr. Stratford, who generally manufactured the most of our small-wit, and who had just come in to take his shovel from the fire. "That's a shovel—a shovel is a shallow iron pan."

" 'From which,' " pursued Lieutenant Sherman, reading, " 'they are removed while still hot, and rolled with the fingers on the palm of the hands, to be brought into the form in which they are found in commerce.' "

"All right," said Mr. Stratford. "You have picked the leaves separately by the hand. I'll dry them artificially by heat in a shallow iron pan, and Sherman can roll them with the finger or in the palm of his hand, to bring them into the right shape."

He drew his shovel from the fire as he spoke, and after knocking off the loose ashes, threw a handful of the yapon leaves upon it.

"These leaves won't roll up," said Lieutenant Sherman, after they had been drying a few minutes on the shovel. "They crack and unroll themselves."

"Yes, but they are old leaves, see how thick they are, and the berries are red and ripe. Here by chance is a young one; the book says, you know, that they value the young leaves most. What better shape could you have than that—just the roll of a tea-leaf."

"And now," said Mr. Stratford, "that they are artificially dried in a shallow iron pan, Sherman, put the coffee-pot on, and let's all take tea."

The turn affairs had taken roused in me rather more than usual curiosity, and as my mug was filled, I examined the tea with rather more than customary care. The aroma was that of poor tea, and the resemblance was quite striking, making me more curious as to the taste. I cooled it down as rapidly as possible and took a sip. There was a woody taste, but through this came the unmistakable flavor of the tea. "Who knows but this is a discovery?" I thought, and so I said emphatically:

"*This is* TEA."

"It is amazingly like it, though not very good."

"It is the tea-plant itself. Sherman, turn back to the article and read the botany."

The lieutenant re-opened the book and again read.

"'The plant which furnishes tea, *Thea Chinensis*, is an evergreen shrub.'"

"This is an evergreen shrub. See how bright the leaves are, though we are near November."

"'Belonging to the class and order *Monadelphia Polyandria*, of the sexual system, and to the natural order *Ternstromiaceæ*.'"

"I think this is Poly—what do you call it?" said Mr. Stratford, encouragingly; "and I'm sure it belongs to the natural order."

"'It is usually from four to eight feet high, though capable, in a favorable situation, of attaining the height of thirty feet.'"

"Texas is a favorable situation," said Lieutenant Sherman. "I can find one that comes up to thirty feet."

"'It has numerous alternate branches.'"

"So has the yapon, alternate and plenty of them."

"'Furnished with elliptical-oblong or lanceolate pointed leaves.'"

"These are elliptical, oblong and pointed leaves."

"'Which are serrate, except at the base.'"

"These are serrate; and let me see, yes, 'except at the base.' Not a saw tooth there."

"'Smooth on both sides, green, shining, marked with one rib and many transverse veins.'"

"'*Smooth on both sides, green, shining, marked with one rib and many transverse veins*'—the exact description. Do look at them."

"'And supported alternately upon short foot-stalks.'"

"'Supported alternately upon short foot-stalks'—so they are."

"'They are two or three inches long and from half an inch to an inch in breadth.'"

"These are little more than half the size. But then the book is describing the cultivated plant, and this is the wild one."

"'The flowers are either solitary or supported two or three together at the axils of the leaves.'"

"What a pity we have not seen the flower!"

"The berries, though, will help us to place them. Here they are 'solitary,' yes, and 'two or three together,' and at 'the axils of the leaves.'"

"'The fruit is a three-celled, three-seeded capsule."

"This has four, but I think that is not material. The

persimmons, for instance, have seven seeds here and only two or three in New Jersey."

"That," said Mr. Stratford, still encouragingly, "is because Texas is such a seedy place. I've grown somewhat seedy myself since I've been here."

"'It is stated that the odor of the tea-leaves themselves is very slight.'"

"The odor of these is *very* slight," remarked Mr. Stratford, "so slight, that I sometimes imagine I don't smell it at all."

"'And that it is customary to mix with them the leaves of certain aromatic plants, such as *Olea Fragrans.*'"

"When the war is over," said Mr. Stratford, in conclusion, "we will get some olea to mix with it, and then it will be all complete. And now let us hurrah for the great American tea. You can stay here and take care of the plant, and I will go home (so soon as I can) and get up a great Texan Tea Company.

VIII.

CAMP FORD.

Autumn was drawing to a close, the leaves had fallen from the trees, the grass was no longer green, and prairie and timber seemed alike bare and cold. Still no exchange had come. We knew of the thirty-seven thousand prisoners taken at Vicksburg, and the six thousand taken at Port Hudson, and therefore we listened hopefully to rumors of exchange, and coined a few of our own, and remained prisoners of war.

Within the prison-camp, affairs had not grown brighter. There was increased sickness with despondency and (for so small a party) many deaths. Two Massachusetts officers had died early. Then the consumptive lieutenant's light had flickered, and with fitful changes grown more and more dim, until it softly expired. A week later, as some of us were awaiting impatiently the breakfast-whistle of our cook, an officer ran hurriedly past to the guard-line, and calling to the surgeon, said, "Come quickly, Doctor, Lieutenant Hayes is dead!" The merry-hearted Irishman lay in his hammock in the composure of an easy sleep. His light had gone out in a single instant. Later, our friend, Mr.

Parce, grew weaker. An order came to send the "citizen prisoners" to Mexico; it did not revive him. His strength waned, but his placid cheerfulness was still undisturbed. "It is a bad sign," said one of his friends, "if he were only cross and fretful, we might hope." The sign did not pass away; and with the prospect of home and liberty held before him he died. We knew that at this rate, another year would leave very few survivors to be carried from the camp.

One gloomy evening, as we sat pondering and talking over our affairs, rumor came in and told us a new tale. It said that the prisoners were to be *paroled* and sent forthwith to the Federal lines. The rumor was confirmed within a day or two by Major Barnes; but when the paroling officer came, it appeared that it was not altogether true; the seamen and privates were to be paroled; the officers were to be sent to Camp Ford.

It behooved us now to find ways and means for carrying our remaining effects to their new abode. By the aid of Major Barnes we succeeded in chartering two wagons for fifteen hundred dollars. We also secured an old hack to carry Mrs. Stratford and four sick officers at fifty dollars apiece. Some of us strove hard to purchase a poor horse or cheap pony that would carry us at any gait. In this race honor compels me to confess that the effrontery of the navy completely distanced the army. Early one morning the camp rang with cries of "Here's yer mule." Through the admiring throng appeared an animal of that description towed in by Captain Dillingham. It was a peculiar animal—small, old, ugly, vicious, and one-eyed. The Captain had bought him on our joint account, and had paid for him one hundred and fifty dollars in the currency of the Confederate States of North America. This alarmingly low price was due to the recent loss of his left optic, causing a dangerous sore, which, the vendor thought, would not prove fatal before we reached Camp Ford. The example was speedily followed by Captain Crocker of the "Clifton," who bought another mule, and by Captain Johnson of the "Sachem," who bought a third, and by Surgeon Sherfy of the "Morning Light," who bought an old "calico" horse that the sailors immediately named "Quinine." The army, either from excess of modesty or excess of poverty, did not succeed, I regret to say, in buying anything.

"Can we ride there on a mule bare-back?" was the question. "Decidedly not," was the answer.

Yet a good saddle in Texas would cost as much as a good horse. In this state of doubt we were relieved by purchasing of a contraband an old wooden "tree" with a strap or two and a piece of raw-hide hanging to it. It bore about the same relation to a saddle that a pair of old wheels do to a cart. But we went to work. And here again the army was eclipsed by the navy. I had been a cavalry officer, and thought I knew a thing or two about broken saddles, and accounted myself fertile in such expedients, but the Captain borrowed a sailor's needle and palm-thimble; brought out an old marlin-spike and some rope, and stitched and spliced with a neatness and rapidity that threw me in the shade. Trunk straps were speedily transferred and changed into girths, some rope was spliced and lashed around a wooden shoe till it became a stirrup, and pieces of raw-hide were bound to the "tree" till it fairly grew to be a saddle.

As the time of departure approached another subject engrossed our attention. Eating continued to be the chief thought and passion of our lives. Whatever could be bought to eat we bought. Our stoves ran literally night and day in baking hard-tack; and we, duly instructed by a professional cracker-baker, pounded dough till our arms ached.

There was still another subject of interest to many. A large part of the officers belonged either to the navy or to new regiments. They were entirely innocent of having slept out a night in their lives, and knew nothing of marches and bivouacs. The fuss which they made about this expected movement was in the highest degree amusing to those who, by virtue of a year or two's service, dubbed themselves veterans. *They* looked on with smiles as they saw the others making good blankets into poor shelter-tents, and winked to each other when they heard the new men confidently assure one another that they could stand it now, even if there should be a wet night upon the march.

After some delay there came in five or six impressed wagons and a squadron of stalwart men mounted on large, well-fed horses. They were chiefly stock breeders from the prairies, and boasted of being the best mounted troop in Texas. All of these men owned the horses they rode, and many brought with them a led horse and servant. They were supposed to be men of unquestionable secession sentiments, and were employed chiefly in hunting down conscripts and guarding prisoners.

On the ninth of December our seamen and privates left us, and we were notified to be ready on the eleventh. Our two wagons came down—a quantity of yapon was gathered and dried—a last baking of biscuit was made, and our stoves were duly incased in open boxes with beckets so as to be readily loaded and unloaded.

A move is always interesting; after months of dreary idleness it is exciting. Happy did we seem, and happy did we feel as on the cold, foggy morning we marched down the "wood-road," crossed the little brook, and left Camp Groce at last behind us. The new Captain—a tall, powerful Texan, with a determined eye and stern, compressed lips—evidently understood his business. He kept us well together, managed his own men with few words and great judgment, and watched the column with close vigilance. The one-eyed mule behaved with gravity and decorum, never showing any unnecessary signs of life or unseemly gayety, except once when he slipped his bridle and ran away like a deer.

Before three o'clock we went into camp on a little brook called "Kane's Creek." Thanks to the autumn rains, there was some water in the "creek," and thanks to the December frosts, it was clear and cold. The proceedings of our naval friends were a new chapter in my experience of bivouacs. Notwithstanding the clear sky and roaring camp-fires, edifices called shelter-tents were erected, with an immense amount of consultation and anxiety. Heavy mattresses were unpacked from the wagons and lugged to the tents. Stoves were unloaded and put up under trees, where they soon smoked and steamed as did the excited cooks who hovered around them. So elaborate, indeed, was the dinner of our mess, that the short winter day closed ere Lieutenant Dane doffed his apron, and summoned us to our seats around the camp-fire. By its light I saw a sirloin of roast beef, a large piece of corned, sweet potatoes, corn bread and butter, flap-jacks and sauce, tea, coffee and cake.

"What are you doing?" asked somebody, as I drew out my pencil and note-book. "I thought you never took notes; it was only an hour ago you were telling me that a note-book spoils a good traveller."

"I am noting down this bill of fare. After my rough experience in our army of the West, this dinner seems too ridiculous to be believed."

"I suppose you will publish it in the newspapers when you get out?"

"Yes, I rather think I shall."

"Well, it's the last of the pepper," said the caterer, "so mind and put it down."

"Yes, by all means."

"And they say we can buy no sugar at Tyler," said another; "so mind and put *it* down."

"Certainly; anything else?"

"There's some salt, and there's a hard-tack. Perhaps you think they are luxuries. And here's a candle, moulded in the neck of a bottle—hadn't you better mention it?"

"I think I had—the mould was so ingenious. You remember I invented it myself."

"You haven't exposed the fact that it's our last pound of coffee, treasured up for this journey?"

"Certainly not."

"Nor that the tea grew in Texas?"

"No."

"Don't—a few such secrets exposed will destroy the whole effect of the bill. And now, if the dinner isn't too much for you, let us box up the stove, while those delicate young gentlemen wash the dishes."

So we boxed up the stove, and washed the dishes, and lit our pipes, and sat looking in the glowing camp-fire. And then our three naval Captains crawled into a tight little shelter-tent, where they suffocated and perspired, and caught cold. The army part of the mess spread their blankets and lay down, with their feet against a smoking log, their heads resting on their knapsacks, and their eyes watching the stars, which twinkled them asleep.

The bugle called us long before daylight to prepare our breakfast and re-load the wagons. I cannot pay Captain Davis a better compliment, than by saying that for five successive mornings we moved off at precisely 6–45, and then for six successive mornings at precisely seven. This day the road ran over some fine rolling country, occasionally clean and park-like, with stately trees sprinkled here and there, and entirely free from young wood and underbrush. The weather was delightful, but we went into camp before two o'clock, after a march of only fourteen miles.

The next morning as we started, a cold gust of north wind struck us. It was not a "norther," but a sudden change of weather from warm to cold. All the morning we breasted it, and it blew keener and keener as the day advanced. Early in the afternoon we encamped in an open wood, which gave but poor shelter from the piercing gale. The little stream that formed our watering place was coated with ice, and the ice grew thicker with each hour. We set ourselves at the work of unloading the wagons and the heavier work of chopping wood for the large camp-fire that must burn all night. The stove went up and puffed and steamed as usual, and all endeavored to impress upon the mind of our amateur *chef* that this extreme cold was only an additional reason that we should eat.

While we were fresh from a sharp walk, with the blood stirred by the active labors of the camp, we were comfortable enough. When we first threw ourselves down before the fire all aglow, saying we were thankful that the work was done, we still felt indifferent to the cold north wind. But presently it crept in, and sent a shivering chill over the frame. Then the nervous energy relaxed, and one felt great need of a warm room where he could hide himself from the blast, and fall asleep if only for an hour. The dinner and the hot tea that accompanied it braced us up somewhat, and fitted us for bed. Our three naval friends again crawled into their shelter tent, where (inasmuch as it was at a prudent distance from the fire) they nearly froze to death. The remainder of the mess used the shelter-tent, a large tree and the stove-box as a wind-break, and put their feet almost in the fire. For some hours we all slept soundly, as men must who have marched and worked since long before day. But although the blankets were drawn over our heads and the wind-break seemed to afford ample protection, the cutting air pushed its way in. It crawled through the hair and curled itself round the neck, and sent the same shivery chills over the body. I rose and warmed myself by rolling a couple of large logs on the fire, and prizing them into their places. The scene around me was wild in the extreme, for every mess had built a large fire, and the flames of these leaped and roared in the blast, and sent large sparks flying through the tree-tops; while in the fiery light, picturesque figures could be seen crouching over the embers or throwing fresh wood into the flames.

The bugle again called us up, while the stars were yet shining, to find the dodger we had baked over night, and the cold beef we had put by for breakfast, frozen harder than paving stones. Close seated by the fire, we ate a moody breakfast, each one declaring that he had not slept one hour during the night, and that he wanted to turn in again. Instead of doing so, we took the road, now solid as a rock. The horses had to stamp through the ice to drink, and the "Sunny South" seemed frozen hard as the hills of the Adirondack.

Passing through Huntsville, we found ourselves upon a sandy road, and travelling through dull woods, whose weary sameness lasted with hardly an interruption for one hundred and fifty miles. Toward evening we encamped beside a deep ravine. The clouds gathered darkly overhead, and the rain began to fall. It bore all the appearances of one of our cold November storms, and we anticipated a tempestuous night. But then came one of the phenomena of the Texan climate. With darkness the rain stopped; and the stars seemed to disperse the clouds. But with daylight the clouds returned, and as we re-commenced the march, the rain came down heavily. The matter was made worse by our immediately descending to the "Trinity bottom," a rich, alluvial plain, three miles in width, composed of the greasiest of mud. When we had dragged ourselves across this, we were suddenly stopped by the Trinity, a narrow stream, deep channelled between precipitous clay banks. A road was cut down each bank, and the usual scow and rope-ferry appeared at the bottom. The prisoners who first arrived on foot were immediately carried over. They scrambled up the opposite bank and instantly made a fire, around which they closely huddled. As the wagons arrived, they were hurried aboard of the scow, for every moment made matters worse. A crowd of men surrounded each wagon as it landed, pushing, pulling, yelling, and in various ways "encouraging the mules." Those extraordinary animals pulled and strained and slipped; now down, now up again, exhausted, and then renewing their efforts, until slowly and inch by inch every wagon was carried to the top of the bank. The scow covered with mules and white-topped wagons, the struggling teams, the shouting men, the howling of the wind, the beating of the rain, all made up a romantic picture. But the toil we paid for it was extreme, and the crossing of this narrow river cost us two hours of time.

We stopped at two houses after crossing, to make some purchases. At the first, the lady of the house (a rather stout female, with a coarse voice and red face) had lost neither children nor relatives in the war, but nevertheless cherished a holy hatred of Yankees. When she learnt that we were of that despised race, and had come into her house to buy something, her wrath became terrific. It even overpowered the irresistible effrontery of the navy. Two of our Captains, who between them had never failed to win the Texan fair, assayed her, but the humor of the one and the blandishments of the other were sent spinning about their ears. "Josiah," she said to her abashed husband, while she quivered with rage, "don't sell them anything, the nasty beasts, I didn't know I hated them so. Don't sell the beasts a thing. Corn meal is too good for them." He, poor man, said "no," but when our two naval commissaries got him alone, they made mince-meat of his scruples in no time. He hurriedly shovelled a bushel of potatoes into their bag, received his five dollars, and begged them to leave by the side door, as most convenient and least exposed to observation.

At the other of these houses, the woman had lost two sons in battle. When she learnt that some of her visitors were enemies and prisoners, she only hastened to express her pity. She spread her simple board with all that her larder contained, and made them sit down. Of some little articles, such as milk and butter and eggs, she literally gave them all she had. Other things that they wished to purchase, she sold—she offered to give, but they forced the money upon her. And when they rose to go, she expressed again her sympathy, and hoped that God would be with them, and comfort them, and send them deliverance.

When we were fairly across the river, and well drenched, the rain stopped, and the freezing north wind began to blow. Colder and colder it grew; and when we passed from the woods to the last prairie we were to see, we had to face a gale. We struggled against this for miles, until, late in the afternoon, there appeared, on the other side of the plain, a little stage-house, and beyond it timber of scraggy trees, small and scattered. It was a poor place to bivouac, but the scarcity of water in this arid country leaves travellers little choice of camping grounds. We halted, therefore, in this bleak spot, and speedily came to the conclusion, that it would be "the coldest night yet." The stove was unloaded as usual, and "put up;" its pipe, lashed to a sapling to keep it from blowing away, and some stove wood chopped. Our indefatigable *chef* then assumed command, and, despite wind and cold, proceeded to roast a lovely loin of delicate pork, purchased of the good woman of the morning, and to serve it up at the proper time with delicious brown crackling and entrancing hot gravy. Before that rapturous moment came there was much work to be done. The wood had to be dragged some distance, for the trees were sparse, and on such a night the fire must be fed with no sparing hand. The water had to be carried, and it was a half-mile distant and at the bottom of a well two hundred feet deep. A tedious job was this, and one that seemed as though it would never end. The pails, the tea-kettle and the iron-pot were all mustered and carried to the well, but others were there before us, and we had to wait our turn. Very slowly the bucket came creeping up while we stood shivering in the wind, and when it appeared it was half empty, and a dozen pails were waiting to be filled before the first of ours. At last when tea-kettle, pot and pails were full, and we were nearly perished, we picked them up and navigated them through the thick brush-wood and against the bitter wind till the ungloved hands were nearly frozen to the iron handles, and the stiff arms ready to drop off. Then, too, our *chef*, like all great artists in that most useful art, was cross, and asked indignantly why we had not come back sooner—if it was so pleasant down at that well that we must stay there all day—if we did not know that nothing could be done without water—if we could not understand that the lovely loin of pork was well nigh spoilt already. We, who were hewers of wood and drawers of water, bore all this meekly and explained. Our *chef*, though an amateur, was about as reasonable as an accomplished female of the same profession, and would hear no explanation. He knew that if *he* had gone *he* would have found a way to get it. We secretly expressed to each other sympathy for scullions, waiters, and other unfortunate persons having business relations with cooks—we crouched down by the fire and thawed our frozen fingers—and then the *chef* sent us back to the well for more water.

> "Now spread the night her spangled canopy,
> And summon'd every restless eye to sleep."

The stove was down and ready to be repacked—the water pails (refilled) stood close before the fire—the stove box, the mess-chest and the shelter-tent again were united for a wind-break—all our night work was done, and there was no reason why we should not sleep. No reason but this bitter north-wind, before which the flames of all the surrounding fires leaned down and the sparks flew level along the ground. And those fires, too, seemed trivial and feeble; the logs that were piled upon them were as heavy as two men could lift, yet were not large enough for such a night as this. Again and again we woke, aching with the cold; and again and again, after crouching over the fire, we returned wearily to our blankets and sought to steal, ere the reveille, a little rest.

> "The purple morning left her crimson bed,
> And donn'd her robe of pure vermilion hue,
> Her amber locks she crowned with roses red
> In Eden's flowery gardens gathered new."

And we resumed the march with blue noses and frosted beards. The wagons rumbled over the frozen ground as upon a rock; the horses shivered and shook more pitiably than their riders. There was unwonted courtesy amongst us. "Do try my mule a little while." "No, I thank you; I could not think of depriving you of him *this* morning." And then the owner, not to be outdone, would dismount, and run along behind his mule with much stamping of the feet and beating of the hands. Comparatively happy then were those wealthy individuals who owned gloves, or who wore something thicker than a summer blouse. Yet the biting air wrought its own cure among the foot passengers and gave them an exhilaration that beat down its benumbing pain; the threadbare, ragged and half-naked crowd, shivering in summer clothing, uttered no whinings, but bravely pushed along, rejoicing that broken boots and tattered garments still held together, and wishing only that they could keep on against the north wind, till they reached the North. Less happy were the few who, seated in the old hack, rode glum and testy with upheaved shoulders and stiff necks, and mile after mile spoke never a word.

Thus, after seven hours' steady marching, we turned

from the road and went down into a little hollow where a small rill furnished us with water, and good large trees with firewood. Here the members of our mess, partly to make up for the previous night, and partly in the hope of attaining comfort, built a fire, which (among themselves) gave to the place the name of the "Camp of the Big Fire."

We were first on the camping ground, and chose our tree, a dry oak more than two feet across the stump. Giving due notice to all that they had better stand from under, the commander of the "Sachem" swung a strong axe against it till it fell. The two largest logs were chopped off, each twelve or fourteen feet long. Skids were cut and laid, and every man, provided with a stiff handspike, lifted and strained till the largest log was raised, "cut round," rolled, re-rolled and placed against its own stump as a brace. The skids were then hauled out and re-laid; and the second log was brought opposite to the first. The skids were next made into an inclined plane, and we, by stout pushing, rolled the second log up this bridge until it rested on top of the first. We then had a solid wooden wall nearly five feet high. In front we placed huge andirons of logs as thick as a man's body. On these we rolled smaller logs, and piled limbs and small wood until the whole sloped down from the top of the wall to a line six or seven feet distant from its base. We worked until the whole tree was in the pile. Then we set fire to it. It kindled slowly, but burnt gloriously. There was no rolling out of our blankets that night to put wood on the fire. We could feel our wooden wall throwing its rays down upon us as we lay before it on the frozen ground. It let no heat pass through, for while one side was a mass of red-hot embers the ice had not melted from the other. We slept until the bugle called us in the morning, and then found that a little rolling together of half-burnt logs and a slight shaking up of unfinished brands gave us a splendid fire to breakfast by.

Thus we went on, until upon the twelfth day of our march we passed through the little town of Tyler and approached Camp Ford. We felt some curiosity as to the appearance and comfort of this new abode. The question put to travellers whom we met always brought the reply that the prisoners were in houses quite comfortable. In houses prisoners might well be comfortable—much better to have houses than the dismal barracks of Camp Groce. At last the road wound round a little knoll, covered with pine and scraggy oak and disclosed the camp. We saw on a side-hill a barn-yard of a place, encompassed by a stockade fence fifteen feet high. Within, partly burrowed and partly built, was an irregular group of log shanties, small, dark and dirty. A naval friend stood at my side, who had been confident that we should find everything to our liking, and whose motto was "Nothing is too good for prisoners." I glanced at him and saw that, since I last looked, his countenance had grown immeasurably longer. A lieutenant of my regiment was on the outside of the stockade waiting to welcome me. He was a young and neat New-Yorker when I last saw him, but his dress now consisted of a pair of ragged trowsers and an old woolen shirt without arms.

"What kind of times have you fallen upon, Mr. L?" I asked.

"Not very good, Colonel," he replied, rather dolefully, and then brightening added, "But we have very good quarters—*at least for prisoners!*"

My naval friend looked at the lieutenant sternly and with disgust. He never forgave that speech.

The roll was called. We were marched forward. The gate opened and admitted us to seven months more of imprisonment. Within every thing looked gloomy and squallid. My own officers I hardly recognized; the others bore in their dress and mien the unmistakable marks of hardship and destitution. A Captain in my regiment came up, and after the usual greetings invited me into his "shebang" and to dinner. I walked in and looked around, I fear with some disgust. A dodger had just been turned out of its pan and cut up.

"I can't stay to dinner, Captain," I said; "we have a wagon to unload; but I'll try a piece of the dodger."

I took a piece and walked out. The gentlemen of the "shebang" said nothing. But afterward there was a story told of the affair. It was this:

"The dodger was the whole of the dinner."

IX.

A DINNER.

The prisoners at Camp Ford were poor. They even thought themselves too poor to borrow. They possessed no supplies to sell; and in manufactures they had not risen above carved pipes and chessmen. They lived on their rations and cooked those rations in the simplest manner. Half of them had no tables, and more than half no table furniture. The plates and spoons did treble duty, travelling about from "shebang" to "shebang" (as they called the hovels they had built) in regular succession.

We rated them soundly about their condition, and asked them why they had lived thus; to which they responded by asking us how they could have lived otherwise. We lectured them severely on their not having begged, and above all, on their not having borrowed; and they answered, meekly, that no one would lend them. We lent them money, but they received it timidly, and expressed fears that they would not be able to re-pay it, and doubts as to whether there was anything to buy. "Nobody ever had anything to sell," they said, "about Tyler."

A few days had passed in the work of improving our "shebang," and we sat one night around the fire moodily, talking over the state of our affairs. We were in the midst of the Christmas holidays, and the contrasted scenes of home pressed rather heavily upon us, and made the present, perhaps, seem darker than it really was.

"Something must be done," said some one, "to raise these fellows up. They are completely *down*, and if we don't get them up, why they will pull us down too."

"I never saw such fellows," said a naval prisoner. "They could have got clothing from the Confederates just as easily as we did. Here we come in, thin and pale and weak, and find them healthy and hearty, and yet all down in their boots. They don't seem to have done anything to keep themselves alive but cook, and not much of that."

"*That's* the remedy," said a third. "You've hit it by accident. 'COOK' is the word. Let us give a dinner-party and astonish them."

"A dinner-party! We *should* astonish them, so that we'd never hear the last of it."

"Well, why not? Didn't some of us 'celebrate' the Fourth at Brashear? and didn't we have a Thanksgiving dinner at Camp Groce? I have great faith in dinners. Why can't we have a New Year's dinner here?"

"For the best of all reasons, because there's nothing to eat. There we had milk and eggs and potatoes and onions and a turkey, and——"

"The turkey was a windfall, and didn't come till we

had determined to observe the day, and Dillingham had issued his proclamation."

"And pumpkin and pecan nuts, and beef."

"Well, I'm sure we have beef."

"Yes, we have, look at the stuff, look at it," and our friend pointed to a dark, dry-looking, fatless lump, that hung from a rafter. "We have got *beef*, and we have got flour, and sugar, and bacon, and those are all."

"Something may turn up if we resolve on it."

"'Something may turn up!' Yes, it may, and when it turns up, we'll give a party."

All agreed to this common sense conclusion, except two obstinate members of the mess, and they were Lieutenant Dane, of the signal corps, and myself.

On the morrow (the thirtieth of December) we went to the gate, presented our compliments to the sergeant of the guard, and informed him that private business with Colonel Allen, commanding, etc., required a personal interview. The sergeant communicated the fact to a gentleman in butternut, who took his rifle and strolled leisurely over to head-quarters with us. The Colonel smiled pleasantly, and as he wrote out the pass, said in a well-bred way, that he never doubted the honor of his prisoners, though he sometimes had a little fear of their discretion, and that when he was applied to by gentlemen who would be discreet in their intercourse with the country people, it afforded him great pleasure to let them out on parole.

The lieutenant and I returned to our quarters, and

hung around our necks a couple of canteens and three or four haversacks; we took a basket and bag, received with gravity sundry bits of ironical advice, and then presenting to the sergeant of the guard our pass, stepped out of Camp Ford on parole.

The road carried us into the woods. At the end of half a mile we descended a hill, crossed a little brook, and found ourselves close upon the white house and negro-cabins of a plantation. At the door we encountered a sour-faced, respectable man, with whom we were soon engaged in the following delightful dialogue:

"Good day, sir."

"Good day."

"Have you any dried fruit to sell?"

"No."

"No apples?"

"No."

"Nor peaches?"

"No."

"Any eggs?"

"No."

"Any chickens?"

"No."

"Couldn't you spare some potatoes?"

"No."

"Nothing to sell for cash, at the highest of prices?"

"No."

"Good day, sir."

"Good day."

It was two miles of dull walking to the next house. A plain-looking old woman appeared and invited us in. As ill-luck would have it, her two sons had been captured at Arkansas Post. Still more unluckily, the two sons, when ill, had been placed in different hospitals, and some surgeon with petty tyranny had refused to let the one brother visit the other. We explained that there were fools in both armies, who treated their own soldiers in the same way. But the old lady said she would forgive everything but that. *That* was unnecessary cruelty. She then heaped coals of fire upon our unoffending heads by presenting to us a pumpkin, and by authorizing her chief contraband, who bore the fruitful name of "Plenty," to sell us from his own private stores a bushel of sweet potatoes. Leaving these treasures till we should return, we went on.

At the third house we had the same conversation over that we enjoyed at the first, and as we turned back into the road it began to rain. "Shall we go back or go on?" was the question. "How far did they say it was to the next house, two miles?" "Yes, two miles. If we go on we shall be wet, perhaps frozen. But no matter; that is better than going back and acknowledging a failure. Come on."

Three miles more, and we came to another house, owned by another old lady. Everything about it was rigidly in order and stiffly neat. There was a startling combination of colors in her parlor; for the floors were unpainted, the walls were white, the ceiling blue, the wainscoting red, and the blinds green. Again we were told that there was nothing to sell. But luckily, at the first item on our list, the old lady's black overseer came in, and being an intelligent contraband, pricked up his ears and asked, what the gentlemen wanted to pay for dried peaches. We inquired what price he asked for them. He reckoned that he had 'bout a peck, and that a peck in these times ought to bring $5; and we thought that $5 was precisely the sum we ought to pay for a peck of peaches. This purchase being happily effected, we ran over the list, but to every item our sable friend "reckoned not," till we mentioned milk. At that liquid name, a thought evidently struck him. He hadn't no milk, but he had vinegar—cider-vinegar—he made it his own self, and he reckoned that in these times it ought to bring $1 a quart. We forthwith entrusted him with every canteen, to be filled full of this precious, and indeed, unrivalled fluid. We then re-applied to the old lady to know whether she really couldn't sell us *something*. But no, not even our free-handed expenditures and the absence of all Yankee cuteness in us, could bring forth the old lady's stores.

As we retraced our steps we noticed a small log-house near the road, and a middle-aged woman barbecuing beef under a little shed. "Let us try here," one of us said; and we went up to the fence and asked for eggs. The woman thought she had a few, and civilly invited us to come in out of the rain. We went in, and found that the house consisted of but one room, and all looked wretched and forlorn. Nearly a dozen eggs were produced, and then the woman bethought herself of a certain fowl that might as well be sold, and set her eldest boys to catch him. A great cackling presently announced the fate of the fowl, and the boys, coming in out of breath, informed us that they had run him down. He was a vagabond-looking young cock, who, any one would swear, ought to come to an untimely end, and I felt a moral pleasure as I tied his legs and popped him into the basket.

And now we had the task of walking six miles back in the rain. As we mounted a rocky ridge we noticed near the road some sumach. The sumach had been so scarce at Camp Groce that we thought this a prize. Setting down our baskets, therefore, we went to work picking sumach, and as we filled our haversacks, we talked of the dinner.

"The last haul is a prize, Colonel," said Lieutenant Dane. "The vinegar is a treasure, and the peaches are worth their weight in Confederate notes. How many shall we ask to dine with us?"

"Yes, it settles the question of dinner. After such luck as this we must go on. I think we can squeeze in six on a side, and one at each end—fourteen in all."

"Fourteen! Well, now, the question is what shall we have? So far our luck is of a very small pattern—a very small pattern indeed. Ten eggs and one chicken of themselves won't make much of a dinner for fourteen men."

"The fact is, we must make this dinner chiefly out of our own brains. Give it the whole weight of your mind; think intensely, and see if you can't hit on a way to make a dish or two out of chips."

"Here's this sumach—what would you make of it?"

"Look at it philosophically. Analyse it: TASTE—*acid;* COLOR—*red.* Now what is there that is acid and red?"

"There are currants for one thing, and there's something else, I'm sure—oh, cranberries."

"Then we must make currants and cranberries out of sumach. But for my part I'm greatly distressed about this wretched fowl—what can we do with him?"

"We might boil him, though he is young and will do to roast."

"What are you thinking of?—one small fowl on a table before fourteen hungry men; ridiculous!"

"Yes, and these healthy fellows have got fearful appetites. They eat like alligators. When they draw three days' beef they devour it in one, for fear (as they say) that somebody might steal it. Can't you make a salad of him such as you used to send over to us at Camp Groce? Do you know when we first came there we all thought the dressing was real?"

"Let us see—we have vinegar, to be sure, and some red peppers. But there is not time now to *manufacture* the mustard, and then we have no milk or butter to make the oil from. No! it's very sad, but we can't have chicken salad!"

"Well, the haversacks are full, so we may as well go on. It rains harder than ever, and that low piece of road will be over our boots in mud and water. I wonder if we shall find the potatoes and pumpkin all safe?"

Our friend "Plenty" duly delivered to us those vegetables when we reached his cabin. Now, a couple of officers trudging along in the mud on a rainy day, laden with a bag of potatoes, a big pumpkin, a couple of overloaded baskets, and several haversacks and canteens, cannot present a very elegant or dignified appearance; nevertheless, a tall man mounted on a ragged-looking steed, and wearing his head stuck through a hole in the middle of his blanket, after the fashion of a Mexican poncha, accosted us as "gentlemen," and in most courteous terms desired to know whether this was the road to Marshall. He gave just one quick, keen glance that travelled all over us, and rested for a single instant on our shoulder straps.

"I perceive, gentlemen," said he, without the slightest diminution of courtesy, "that you belong to the other side."

I nodded an assent.

"And that you are officers?"

I nodded again.

"I presume you are prisoners then, and here on parole?"

Now, wearing a United States uniform at that time in Texas by no means proved that a man was in the United States service; it only indicated that he was a soldier.

So many prisoners were in *their* butternut, and so many Confederates in *our* uniform that a Texan eye rarely looked behind the coat to distinguish the kind of soldier it covered. When, therefore, our tall friend said, "You are on the other side," and added, "you are officers," it was plain to us that he had made the close acquaintance of our troops in some other way than through the newspapers.

"I perceive that you are an old soldier," I said in reply. "And I do not think you are a Texan. Allow me to ask where you are from?"

"I belong to the 1st Missouri Cavalry," said he, "and I am from Missouri."

"From Missouri!" I exclaimed. "Why, I was in service there myself during the first year of the war."

The tall man and I looked steadily at each other in mutual astonishment. The same thoughts were passing through our minds, and he expressed them first and best by saying:

"You know, sir, that if you and I had met this way in Missouri, that first year of the war, only one of us would have walked away, and maybe neither."

"Yes," I said, "the war was very bitter there."

"It was that. No man could have made me believe then that I could ever meet an enemy with the same friendly feelings I have for you, gentlemen."

Here our friend began to unbuckle his saddle-bags, and after much trouble produced a flat bottle. "A friend," he said, "gave me this, and I mean to carry it through to Arkansas, if I can, but I must take a drink with a gentleman that was on the other side in Missouri, the first year of the war, if I never drink again as long as I live."

We touched our lips to the detestable poison, and thanked our friend for his courtesy. The "border ruffian" then expressed his great satisfaction at finding we were treated as gentlemen and prisoners of war should be, and said he doubted if he didn't respect the soldiers on "the other side" rather more than he did a good many folks on his own. Finally he asked our names—gave us his own, which was Woodland—shook hands warmly, and rode off. We shouldered our loads and plodded on, wondering whether the barbarous and brutal trade of war does not of itself inspire men at last with some noble and chivalric sentiments.

These meditations lasted us till we reached the gate. We were somewhat apprehensive that our appearance would produce a sensation in camp, and excite anticipations of the coming festivities, but luckily the rain and cold had driven all within their hovels. We walked rapidly past the closed doors of the "shebangs" till we hastily kicked open our own, and threw down our loads before the eyes of our astonished messmates. Then after a savage attack on cold beef and hot dodger, and after brewing a hot decoction of sumach to keep the cold out, we hung our wet clothes before the fire, and rolled ourselves in our warm blankets for the rest of the evening. Ere we fell asleep some one came in and said that it was freezing, and that the ground was white with snow.

The ground was white with snow, and so were our

blankets the next morning. The north wind blew a gale—a goodly sized snow-drift stretched across the floor of the "shebang"—the water pail was frozen nearly solid, and a cup of sumach tea that stood upon the table directly in front of the fire was coated with ice. Daylight stole in through many chinks and crevices to find us still shivering in our bunks. One gentleman suggested that another gentleman rise and cook the breakfast; but the other gentleman thought the day would be long enough if we had breakfast any time before sunset. A humorous man from another "shebang" poked his head in the door, and inquired whether we would like to be dug out in the course of the day. We took no notice of his humor, and shivered in silence. At length the most uncomfortable one rolled out, threw a pile of logs upon the fire, and swept away the snow. As a matter of course the others followed. Breakfast was first disposed of, and then Lieutenant Dane began his great work. All of that day we were engaged, like Count Rumford, on a series of scientific experiments closely allied to the art of cookery. When night came we had fought our way over all obstacles, and were able to announce that the dinner should come off and should be a success.

The two junior members of the mess had at the outset agreed (in bad faith) that if we would cook the dinner, they would wait upon the table. We now held them to this agreement, and, as a righteous punishment for their contempt, determined to cut the dinner up into as many courses as we decently could, and make them wash the plates at the end of every course. The rest of the mess who had been abashed by our foraging and overawed by our experiments, became gradually interested, and joined in the work by inviting the guests, manufacturing a table, and chopping an immense pile of wood for the evening.

"Happy New Year's" came to us bright and clear, and the prisoners followed the old Dutch custom by wandering around and wishing each other happier returns of the day. At our "shebang" we were compelled to inform visitors that we received on the other side of the way. We were, in fact, busy beyond powers of description, scolding, as I have observed good cooks always scold, and ordering in the style that really talented artists always order. We had three fires in full blast—one in our fire-place, one in our stove, and one under an independent pot. I observed, I regret to say, that one or two of the invited strolled up with a suspicious air, as if they really feared the invitation might be what the vulgar term "a sell," and the dinner so much moonshine. It was plain that they were not used to being invited out. As the appointed hour approached, the remarks of passers-by gradually called our attention to the fact that this was the coldest day ever known in Texas. (4° Fahr.) Some extra work was therefore necessary. We placed the table across the "shebang" directly in front of the fire-place, and close behind the table, hung blankets from the roof to the floor, thus curtaining out the cold after our Camp Groce plan. There were actually found crockery platès in camp just sufficient to go round, and also two naval table-cloths, which spliced, exactly covered the table. We devoted our last three candles to illume the festal board; and we built a fire over a back-log as large as a barrel.

As the hour of six o'clock approached our guests were adroitly intercepted at the door, and carried into a neighboring cabin, where they were entertained till wanted. When every thing was ready, the last finishing touches given, and the two waiters fully instructed with respect to some strategic movements to be executed behind a curtain, the door was opened, and our guests triumphantly marshalled in. As these misguided men, who for half a year had been devouring rations off of tin plates, and had not so much as heard the word table-cloth spoken—as they descended into the "shebang," they seemed to be fairly dazed with the splendors of the apartment. They sank into their designated seats, too much appalled to speak, and only talked in subdued tones after three or four courses. The first course was on the table. It consisted of soup and wheaten bread—flour bread, as it was vulgarly called in camp. I observed—at least I had a sort of suspicion—that one or two of the guests had an habitual idea that soup was all the dinner; for they looked nervously over their shoulders when an adroit waiter (with an eye to the morrow,) whisked the soup off the table immediately after everybody had been helped *once*.

The *soup* plates were removed by one waiter: he disappeared with them behind the curtain, and re-appeared with the dinner-set in about the time the other waiter had placed the second course upon the table. It might have been remarked that our soup plates were rather shallow, and our dinner plates, by contrast, rather deep; but the eyes of our guests were too dazzled to perceive such slight peculiarities. We knew that it was a wise maneuvre to show great profusion at the beginning of a dinner. The guests then have their anxiety allayed, and carry with them an overpowering idea of plenty, which of itself allays the appetite. Accordingly we double shotted this gun. At the head of the table appeared a dish not generally known or appreciated. Sweet potatoes and beef entered largely into its composition. A hungry naval officer had introduced it into the mess, and he called it *scouse.* Yet it served a certain purpose well, and was skilfully slipped in at this point to attract the attention of gentlemen with vigorous appetites. At the other end appeared a broiled spare-rib, and the lines of communication between these right and left wings were kept open by detachments of squash, turnips, boiled potatoes, and *cranberry* sauce. With secret pleasure we saw our friends lay in heavily of the scouse, and deceive themselves into the foolish belief that we had thrown two courses together, and that this was the dinner.

But the next course came on, with clean plates, in the imposing form and substance of a Chicken Pie. A magnificent chicken pie it was, filling an immense pan, and richly crowned with brown crust heaving up above the brim. It had no accompaniments save baked potatoes, and constituted of itself an entire army corps. No one associated with it the idea of anything little, or niggardly, or economical. On the contrary, all applauded it enthusiastically, and declared that it alone would have made a dinner.

From the gravity of this heavy dish we passed to the gayety of mince and pumpkin pies. These were the only common-place things in the dinner. They were followed by a course of tarts—small, refined-looking tarts, elegantly covered with currant jelly and beautiful pear preserves. This course was surprisingly showy and genteel, impressing beholders with the idea that there must be a pastry-cook shop concealed somewhere in the camp. Our grand climax was one of those efforts of genius sometimes called "jelly-cake," sometimes "Lafayette cake," sometimes "Washington pie." It was some eighteen inches in diameter, and four or five inches thick, (the exact size of our dodger pot), a beautiful brown on the outside, and a rich golden yellow within, and when cut was seen to be divided by strata of tempting jelly. Finally, we closed with coffee (not corn, but Java) and tea (not Thea Chinensis, but Thea Texana), and tobacco inhaled through pipes, instead of through the original leaf. We broke up, after the usual four hours' sitting of a respectable party, with the usual courtesies and ceremonies. One or two late men stayed, as they always do, to tell their best stories; and one or two early men slipped off, as they always do, on the plea of domestic engagements. There was one or two small mishaps, such as a slight infusion of red pepper in the coffee (occasioned by one of the cooks grinding the pepper first), and the house getting a-fire (caused by the stoker piling the wood as high as the log mantel), but the affair, as a whole, was a grand, noble, philanthropic success.

For the benefit of those persons who (allured by the brightness of this report) desire to become prisoners, I will minutely narrate how this wonderful result was obtained.

The soup was *real*, and probably the strongest thing of the kind ever made, for a choice assortment of beef-bones were boiled for thirty-six hours. The turnips and spare-rib were a present from the Confederate Commissary, Lieutenant Ross, and came in the very nick of time. That solitary fowl we had discussed for a mile or two of our walk back, and had finally determined to put him in a pie. But the only pie-dish we could procure was a large tin milk-pan. To have a dish half full of pie would never do. It was necessary both to have pie enough and to fill the dish. From Confederate beef we selected pieces free from fat and grizzle, and then took the fowl and chopped him up bones and all. The beef was also chopped, and the two mixed thoroughly together. The fragments of bone, to which some prejudiced housewives would have objected, were of great value to us in establishing the authenticity of the pie; for a man who, with every mouthful he took, pricked his tongue on a splinter of chicken bone, could not doubt (if he were a reasoning creature) that he was eating chicken pie.

The next, and perhaps the greatest achievement of our art, was in the currant and cranberry line. We made, after many experiments, a strong decoction of sumach. Into this we stirred flour, slightly browned to reduce its color and take off the raw taste. When this mixture was properly sweetened and cooled it made a dark, pasty substance, looking and tasting precisely like poor currant jelly. The cranberry sauce was more difficult, and involved repeated experiments. Finally a handful of dried peaches was chopped up, so that when cooked the pieces would appear about the size of cranberries. To get rid of their peach flavor, we soaked them and boiled them and drained the water off, and then cooked them slightly in a decoction of sumach, and added sugar in the usual way. Although every one must have known that there were no cranberries in Texas, yet no one dared to question the reality of this dish. It was not cranberry, but it was so like cranberry that they could not imagine what else it could be, and feared to betray their ignorance.

A shrewd observer will have noticed the fact that our invaluable peaches nowhere appeared on the bill of fare. Indeed they were very carefully kept out of sight, and did duty in the secret service. Those mince pies! They were made of peaches—of peaches and mince-meat, well flavored, and moistened with cider-vinegar. I cannot assert that they were poor, for we had no other mince-pies wherewith to compare them; I cannot deny that they were good, because they were all eaten up. The proof was in their favor.

The big pumpkin that we carried under one arm till benumbed, and on one shoulder till a stiff neck for life threatened us, was a very useful vegetable. In one course it appeared as squash; in another as pumpkin, and in a third as pear. The chief cook recollected hav ing seen or heard of pumpkin preserves, and our early experiments pointed to ultimate success. To succeed, however, the simplest common sense told us we must have a name for our invention. To call it *pumpkin sweatmeats* would ruin it. We knew that guava jelly and preserved ginger must become bankrupt under such a label. Accordingly we cut the pumpkin in pieces, like those of a quartered pear; we stewed it till it was not quite done (a little tough where the core ought to be); we spiced it with sassafras, prickly-ash, a few cloves, and the last half of a nutmeg, and we called it pear-preserve.

It will be remembered that I alluded to a gigantic cake, beautifully brown without and richly yellow within. This magnificent work of art, truth compels me to say, was a failure. Its golden richness was not due to eggs but to corn-meal. We mixed a dodger with some flour, to give consistence, and some sugar, to give sweetness. We baked it at the right time and in the right manner. We sliced it up, and daubed the slices over with artificial currant jelly. We went a step farther, and called it cake. We even varied the name of the cake, to meet the prejudice or fancy of the particular guest about to be helped. But vulgarly speaking, "it was not a go." We could cheat our guests through the medium of their eyes and ears in many things, but we couldn't cheat them on dodger. When they tasted dodger, they recognized dodger. Dodger for breakfast, dodger for dinner, and dodger for supper, in the course of half a year, makes a deep impression on the human mind. A little sugar and jelly were wholly inadequate to smooth it away. Here, then, in the very flush of victory, we were in danger of suffering a shameful defeat. Earlier in the dinner we could have brought up fresh forces, but now, in the hope of making the affair overwhelming, we had thrown our last reserve into action. A retreat was ruin, and an instant of hesitation would have acknowledged a defeat. In less than an instant we turned the retreat into a flank movement. Captain Dillingham, with naval effrontery, gave the cake a new name, and called it a JOKE!

Thus ended this great dinner. Our guests retired from it wiser and better men. A profound sensation was followed by a healthy excitement. Manufactures sprang up and trade began. Some gentlemen made caps from rags, and hats from straw. Others built a gymnasium for amusement, and others engaged in gardening for recreation. A few musicians manufactured banjoes, tanning the parchment and preparing the strings in camp. One officer, possessed of a worn-out file, a large screw, and a couple of old horse-shoes, ground the file into a chisel, and turned the screw and worn-out horse-shoes into a good turning lathe. Another changed this lathe from half-action to full-action. A third made for it a crank and foot-treadle. A fourth built an entirely new lathe, better than the first. And thus affairs went on until we numbered more than forty articles of camp manufacture made, chiefly, like our dinner, out of nothing.*

* Among these fabrics manufactured and sold by the prisoners in Texas, were:

Axe helves, Baskets, Blacking, Brooms, Candles (mould and dip), Chairs (arm and rocking), Chessmen, Checkermen, Crockery-ware, Caps (military), Cigars, Door mats, Hats (straw); Musical instruments, viz., banjoes, castanets and triangles; Pails, Pepper-boxes, Pipes, Potash, Rings, Shirt-studs, Sleeve-buttons, Soap, Shoes, Tables, Toy-boxes; Wooden-ware, viz., knives, forks, spoons, plates, dishes, bowls, salt-cellars, wash-boards.

X.

ESCAPE.

THROUGH illness, changes, toil and trouble, the subject of escape never left our minds. At Camp Groce, weakness and ill-health constantly postponed intended attempts. Moreover, the open prairie country around the camp, the nearness of the coast-guard, and, above all, the absence of any point or outlet to which to run, were disheartening obstacles. At Camp Ford, it was somewhat different; for the woods came down nearly to the stockade, and the country was one vast forest.

The troubles that beset the path of an escaping prisoner in Texas were entirely different from those which would attend him in the Northern States. The difficulty of passing the stockade and guard was trivial; the difficulties of crossing the surrounding country were not insurmountable; but after hundreds of miles were traversed, and weary days and nights had exhausted the body and dulled the mind, then the chief obstacles began. Two hundred miles to the south was the Texan coast-guard. One hundred and fifty miles to the east were the carefully watched lines of the Red River and Atchafalaya. To the north were the rebel Cherokees and the open Indian country. Five hundred miles west of us stretched desolate prairies, and beyond them were the scouts that watched and guarded the Rio Grande. In short, when we studied the map, we saw no city of refuge to which we might flee; when the stockade was scaled and the pursuit evaded, there was still no outlet of escape. Further than this, the chances of re-capture were many. To look over the wide extent of country with its sparse population, its scattered plantations, its remote towns, and talk of pursuing prisoners would seem as idle as searching for needles in a haystack. But every road was watched, every river was guarded. Every man or woman or boy who was not a secret Unionist was in effect a Confederate patrol; the entire State was one great detective police, constantly pursuing prisoners, refugees and slaves.

Yet, after calmly contemplating these difficulties, the greater part of the prisoners at Camp Ford determined to escape. Perhaps the determination was quickened and extended by annoyances which began soon after our arrival, and which steadily increased. There are said to be "bad streaks" in all countries, and Tyler is situated in a very bad streak of Texas. The inhabitants were poor, ignorant and narrow-minded, and viewed, with angry ill-will, the liberality of Colonel Allen. They poured in complaints at head-quarters, and the result was, that one fine morning, the poor Colonel received a reprimand for his liberality, and strict orders not to let us out of the stockade.

The kindness of Colonel Allen and his amiable wife

was not lessened by its unpopularity. Regularly, every afternoon, Mrs. Allen came within the stockade, accompanied by a little black girl bearing a basket. Sometimes she brought in visitors, partly to amuse us and partly to soften them. She was tireless in every work that could add to our comfort. She cheered the despondent and comforted the weak, and for the sick, showed that beautiful solicitude that no one save a Christian woman can evince.

There was a little paper then in camp, printed with the pen by Captain May, of the 23d Connecticut, which was read successively in the "shebangs," and shortened the hours and occupied the mind. It had much *local* wit and humor, but so blended with the inner life of Camp Ford, that the outside world can never understand its hits and jests. Yet frequently the "Old Flag" rose above satire and humor, and it enabled Lieutenant-Colonel Duganne to pay to Mrs. Allen the following graceful tribute:

"ALL kindly acts are for the dear Lord's sake,
And His sweet love and recompense they claim:
'I was in prison'—thus our Saviour spake,
'And unto me ye came!'

"So, lady! while thy heart with mother's love
And sister's pity cheers the captive's lot,
Truth keeps her record in the courts above,
And thou art not forgot.

"Though nations war, and rulers match their might,
Our human bosoms must be kindred yet,
And eyes that blazed with battle's lurid light,
Soft pity's tears may wet.

"Were all like thee, kind lady, void of hates,
And swayed by gentle wish and peaceful thought,
No gulf would yawn between contending States,
No ruin would be wrought.

"May all thy matron's heart, with joy run o'er
For children spared to bless thy lengthened years—
Peace iu thy home, and plenty at thy door,
And smiles, to dry all tears.

"And may each cheering hope and soothing word
That thou to us sad prisoners hast given,
Recalled by Him, who all our prayers hath heard,
Bring the reward in Heaven."

When the minds of many men are given wholly to one subject, it is incredible how many expedients they can devise. Yet no expedient could be devised to comply with one condition which the calmer judgments imposed, and which was thus allegorically expressed by one of our friends in the guard, "When General Green spreads his tents, there will be plenty of good recruits join him;" which meant, "You had better wait till the leaves are out."

At length, in the latter part of March, ere the buds were fully blown, the impatience of fifteen officers broke through their discretion. They divided into three parties, and made their preparations carefully. Old haversacks were mended, and new ones made. Suspicious articles of dress were exchanged. Some beef was saved and dried; hard-tack was baked, and panola made. This last article was recommended by the Texans. It consists of corn-meal browned to about the color of ground coffee, with a liberal allowance of sugar stirred in. Its advantages are that it requires no cooking, and contains a large amount of nutriment in proportion to its bulk and weight.

The parties were soon ready to start. But the Texan atmosphere is dry and clear, with cloudless nights. One evening, while the colors of sunset were still glowing upon the western sky, an officer came to me, and pointing to a black cloud that was rising from the horizon, said, "If that cloud comes up overhead, we will make the attempt." It was a bad hour, in every way; for darkness had not yet succeeded day, and the moon was already throwing her pale light upon the eastern clouds. Yet this cloud might not come again for weeks, and its dark shadow was too precious to be lost.

A gay party assembled in the "shebang" nearest to the southern side of the stockade. They had a fiddle and banjoes and castanets, and all the vocal minstrelsy of the camp. They roared Irish songs, and danced negro break-downs, and the little cabin shook with the tumult of their glee. Down at the farther corner of the enclosure, where all was gloom and quiet, two men crawled on the ground to the stockade. They were about thirty feet apart, and a rope lay between them. The sentry on the outside heard the merriment in the "shebang," and as all was quiet on his beat, he walked up to look at the Yankee's fun. He passed the two men. The second twitched the rope; the first quickly rose, and dug with all his might. A few minutes, and the hole was deep enough to allow a post of the stockade to be canted over, so as to leave a narrow aperture between it and its neighbor. The man laid down his spade, signalled to some one behind him, and began to squeeze himself through the opening. Fourteen others rose from the ground, and one by one, trembling with impatient eagerness, pressed through and followed him. They crossed the sentries' path, ran up a little hill that fronted the stockade, and disappeared beneath the trees beyond. The second of the two men still lay upon the ground. The last of the fifteen was to have twitched the rope, and this man was to have replaced the post. But who, at such a time, ever looked behind to see if he were last? The signal was not given! Within the "shebang" still rose the racket, and still the sentry stood grinning at the Yankee antics. But from the other direction came the tramp of the next guard-relief!

Among those who waited and listened, and saw nothing, there was intense suppressed excitement. In vain one or two moved round, begging the little groups to break up—to stifle their earnest whispers—to resume the ordinary hubbub of the evening—to laugh—to sing—to do anything. In vain a young lieutenant, who was both a wit and vocalist, burst forth with—

"Roll on, silver moon!
Light the traveller his way."

The groups broke up, but re-formed; the whispers stopped for a moment, and then went on.

The corporal of the guard halted his relief, and could be seen observing the opening of the leaning post. There was a little pause, and then a light came down to the suspicious opening. There was a little longer pause—a slight stir through the guards' quarters, and then a squadron of cavalry rode out, and an officer, with four or five men, went at a gallop down the Tyler road.

The black cloud seemed to be the fugitives' friend; for at this moment of discovery it poured down a heavy shower. We retired to our cabins, and felt some little relief in the hope that the friendly cloud had washed away the trail. Some time passed—perhaps two hours, and our hope had well-nigh turned into belief; when, from the Tyler road, a low, wailing, ominous cry smote upon our ears. "Did you hear that?" each asked of the other, in startled whispers. "Yes; the *blood-hounds!*"

The hounds came down to the stockade. They snuffed and moaned for a moment around the opening, and then ran straight up the bank and under the trees. There lay the trail. We listened until their faint baying could be heard no longer. Of all the dismal sounds that mortal senses were ever laden with, none more melancholy than the baying of these hounds was ever heard. We passed the uneasy night in speculating upon the chances of the three parties, and in trying to imagine the feelings of our friends when they should first hear the foreboding wail behind them, and surmise that the bloodhounds were upon their track.

Yet the next morning the prospect appeared brighter. Three showers of rain had fallen during the night; twelve hours had passed since the escape, and we felt confident that the hounds must have lost the scent. The day passed in growing cheerfulness, and at taps no tidings had come. We went to our quarters, sure that all had been successful. About nine o'clock that evening, the door of my "shebang" opened, and Lieutenant-Colonel Leake, of the 20th Iowa, entering, presented, with mock formality, Lieutenant Lyon, of the 176th New-York. He and his party had been recaptured.

There were still eleven officers out, who, we knew, were divided into two parties. Twenty-four hours must have passed before the hounds could have taken their trail, and every hour dissipated the scent. The second day passed without news. So did the third evening, and the morning of the third day. Then, about noon, word was passed in from the guard-house that nine more were caught.

In an hour or two, they came, close packed on the bottom of a wagon. We waited with some anxiety the reception they would meet with at head-quarters. Colonel Allen came out, shook hands with one or two, laughed, and manifestly treated the affair as a joke. The wagon started for the gate. Its way lay through the quarters of the guard, who had, of course, turned out to look at the runaway Yanks. We waited in the painful expectation of hearing a Texan yell over the misfortune of our friends. To their honor be it known, the Texans showed no ill-mannered exultation. But the instant it was settled that no shout of triumph was to be raised by the victorious rebs, there was a revulsion of feeling in the prison community. As the gate opened, a slight, restless stir ran through the crowd. As the wagon drove in, a loud shout arose (couched in expressive Texan slang) of, "Here's your mule! Here's your mule!" The runaways smiled feebly, as men do who are the victims of a joke. The crowd laughed boisterously, and gave excellent imitations of the baying of hounds. About the same time, a little three-year-old, the child of a commissary-sergeant, came out on the bank opposite to us, and in shrill tones piped out, "Yankee ran away! Yankee ran away!" And all the afternoon, the little wretch would come, at short intervals, and re-sing his refrain, "Yankee ran away! Yankee ran away! Yankee ran away!"

When we came to collate the stories of the three parties, and of their captors, we gathered the following account: each party had kept secret its intended movements; yet all had selected substantially the same route. Unluckily for them, their trails crossed, and, still more unluckily, there rode with the Confederates an old western trapper, whom the men called Chillicothe. When the first party was captured, the pursuers merely returned to the crossing of the second trail, and followed it up In like manner, when they had captured the second party, they only came back to the third trail. At these crossings, the prisoners could see nothing; but to the eyes of Chillicothe and the instinct of the dogs, the two trails were as plain as the crossings of two streets. The trapper told the prisoners where they had been, and nearly everything they had done. He showed them where (unknowingly) they entered a swamp by the same opening, and crossed a stream on the same tree. He pointed out to them the spot where they sat down to rest, and the hill up which one climbed to reconnoitre. He described to them a log where one pulled off his boots, and another lit his pipe. A secret history of their movements seemed to be written upon the ground.

The story of the last party captured was this: they marched rapidly all of the first night, and hid themselves through the first day. At dark, they resumed their march, and continued to travel rapidly through the woods. On the second morning, they selected, as a hiding-place, a narrow gully, roofed over and completely hidden by a fallen tree. The barking of dogs and crowing of cocks told that a plantation was near. In the afternoon, two restless members of the party insisted on going there to buy eggs. Hardly had they gone, when, in the opposite direction, was heard the baying of hounds. Yet there were no fears of being tracked, for forty-four hours had passed since the party left camp. The baying came nearer. Still it was thought that a party of hunters were accidentally coming that way. A number of horsemen rode down to the little brook at the foot of the hill, and paused there to water their steeds. The dogs, at the same time, started, and came directly up the hill. A beautiful dark hound led the pack, and when he reached the tree, he mounted it with his fore-feet, and looked intelligently down on the prisoners. They remained quiet, fearing that some growl or bark might betray them, yet hoping the hounds would pass on. The leader turned, and quietly trotted down the hill. He went, not to his owner, but to the lieutenant who commanded the party; he looked a moment at him, and then turning looked toward the fallen tree. The lieutenant instantly shouted, "Here they are!" All of his men drew their pistols, and spurred their horses up the hill. The tree was surrounded, and the fugitives recaptured.

What became of the two remaining officers was a question with us for many weeks. The unerring hounds had started on their trail, but the lieutenant who commanded, had ordered that they should be called off. He did not know how many prisoners had escaped, and moreover, he had already caught two parties of four each. Therefore, when he found five prisoners in the gully, he naturally concluded that they were all. Several weeks after this, a quotation from a New Orleans paper assured us of their safe arrival within our lines.

The first fact impressed upon us by these adventures was the wonderful power and sagacity of the blood hounds. During the next three months, a long list of experiences re-taught this lesson. The Confederates possessed in them "pursuing angels," whose powers exceeded those of men. If you buried yourself in the earth, they dug you out. If you climbed a tree, they came and stood at the foot. If you plunged into trackless wilds, they followed you. If you threw yourself into a stream, and threaded its windings for miles, they passed tirelessly up and down its bank, until they came to the spot where you had left it. As every means that ingenuity could devise failed, and as prisoner after prisoner who tried them was recaptured, there gradually grew up, in our minds, a feeling that to be hunted by these brutes was like being pursued by dreadful phantoms, such as we read of in old stories, which no mortal power could outstrip or elude, if their insatiate chase once began.

At the time of the escape of the fifteen, a number of officers were secretly engaged in "tunnelling out." There were two plans connected with this tunnel. The first was that all who wished to escape should pass out on the same night and then scatter in small parties. We knew that some of these parties would be caught—we also thought that some would escape, and every man hoped that he would be in a lucky party. The second plan rested in the breasts of but three or four officers, and they hardly ventured to speak of it to each other. It was that on some dark night we would pass all able-bodied men out, form them in the neighboring woods, march boldly down the road, and surprise the guard in their quarters; then after burning the Confederate arsenal and workshops at Tyler, we would seize upon horses sufficient to mount the party, and push without ceasing for the Sabine and our lines beyond.

About one hundred feet beyond the north side of our enclosed camp stood two large trees. The spot was known as the "Quartermaster's Grave," for there slept Lieutenant John F. Kimball, Quartermaster of the 176th New York. The grave, carefully enclosed by a wicker fence, was between the two trees. The sentries' walk was close to the stockade and parallel to the grave. Within our enclosure the "shebangs," though not built upon any plan, had nevertheless sprung up with somewhat of the regularity of streets. One, however, called from its Indiana owners, the Hawk-eye, stood detached, and only about sixteen feet from the stockade. This cabin was taken for our starting point. In one corner a shaft was sunk eight feet in depth and length by four in width. From the bottom of this shaft the tunnel started. It was just high enough for a man to sit erect and work, and just wide enough for two men to meet and pass by each other. Two men worked in it at the same time, the one excavating and the other removing the earth. Their tools consisted of an old sword-bayonet, a broken shovel and a small box.

The first difficulty met was in establishing the grade and direction of the tunnel. The top of it at the shaft was less than five feet below the surface, while the posts of the stockade stood four and a half feet deep. It was necessary to go well below them, and therefore necessary to start with a descending grade. Beside the Quartermaster's grave were three others. They projected over a line drawn from the shaft to the largest tree, and we designed that the tunnel should come out through the roots of this tree like a fox-earth. The wicker fence with the trunk and shadow of the tree, formed so perfect a screen from the sentries that a hundred men could have passed out on a stormy night with only remote chances of detection. Yet as the graves projected over the line I have mentioned, it was necessary for us to deflect from our true course until we should pass them, and then turn and work toward the tree. To bore under ground in the dark, and hit such a mark as the tree could not be done by chance or guess-work. We also must know the exact distance of the point where we should turn from our deflecting course; for if we turned too soon we should run into the graves, and if we turned too late we should shoot beyond the tree.

The difficulty of grade and direction was speedily disposed of. A pocket-compass and a small vial were soon procured, and Mr. Johnson, engineer of the gun-boat "Diana," with admirable skill combined them into a good surveyor's compass and level. The direction of the tree was taken, the amount of our deflection estimated, and the compass-level handed to the workmen with orders to keep on a certain grade and course.

To ascertain the exact distance of the tree was a harder task. For this three methods were suggested. It was first proposed that an officer should go out for wood, and as he passed this part of the stockade, some one should request him to copy the inscription on a head-board. He would then come up to the stockade for a pencil, and thence walk directly to the tree, counting his steps as he went. The objection to this was that it might excite suspicion, and draw attention to the tree.

The second method was to form an interior triangle, which should be equal to an imaginary exterior triangle. To do this it was indispensable that we should have "a given angle" and a "given side" of each. Our pocket-compass was too small to take angles, and moreover this had to be done literally within a few inches of the sentries and before their eyes. It was advisable, therefore, to measure and establish our given angle without instruments, and in the most artless manner.

Now every body possessed of a smattering of geometry knows that in a right-angled triangle the square of the hypothenuse is equal to the sum of the squares of the other sides. Yet very few people can turn that knowledge to any practical account. This theorem, however, enabled us readily and accurately to establish a right-angle, and to use it as our "given angle." It was done in this way: we took a cord and measured off and marked with pins, ten feet, eight feet, and six feet. By squaring these numbers it will be seen that $10^2=8^2+6^2$. Hence by bringing our line into the shape of a triangle (the pins designating the angles), we formed of it a right-angled triangle.

It was not to be supposed that a Texan sentry, seeing us measuring with a cord on the inside of the stockade, would ever dream that we were measuring distances on the outside. Yet it was desirable that our measurements should be few and quickly done. After thus marking the line, and also measuring upon it twenty feet, Captain Torrey, of the 20th Iowa and myself, carried it up to the Hawk-eye cabin, dropped it on the ground, and quickly

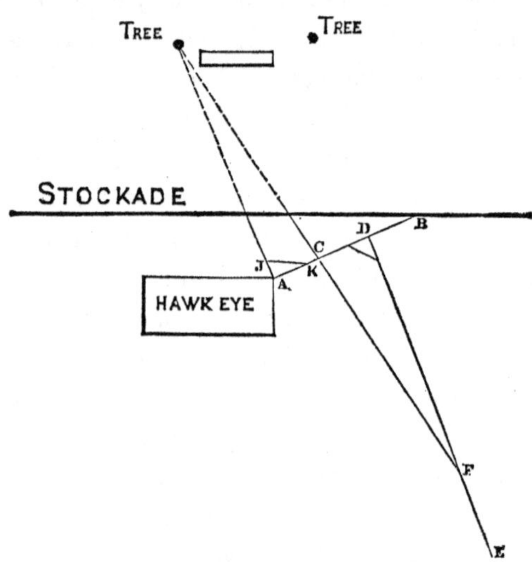

drew it into the form of the little triangle—A J K. As soon as the side A J came on a line with the tree, one of us glanced along the other side A K and noted the point B where its projection struck the stockade. He then quickly measured twenty feet in this direction, and stuck a peg in the ground at C. He measured twenty feet more and placed another peg at D. Here we re-set the triangle, which gave us the new direction D E. One of us then walked down this course till he found himself on a line with the peg C and the tree.

Here we placed another peg, F. We then picked up the cord and came away. When the guard was relieved, and a new set of sentries stood around the stockade, we went back and measured the distance from F to D. It was equal to the distance from the cabin to the tree.

The third method was suggested by Captain Torrey. It was to take the altitude of a triangle by trigonometry. A table of logarithms remaining in the possession of a naval officer, enabled us to do this. Captain Torrey laid off the base of his triangle well down in the camp, out of sight of the sentries. To measure the angle at A he

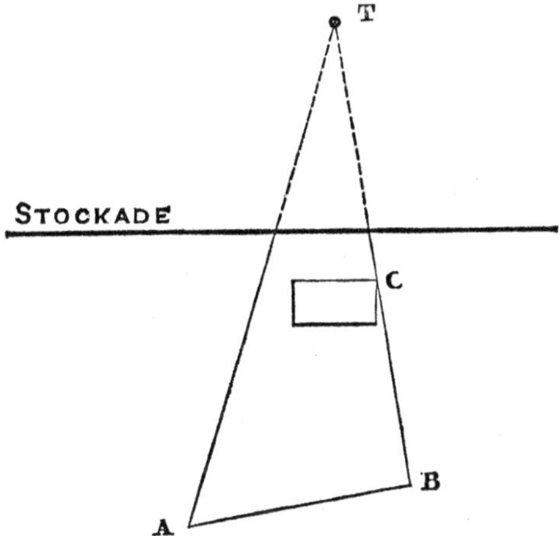

described a circle on the back of a large chess-board, and divided it as accurately as he could into degrees. When the altitude B T was thus obtained, all that remained necessary to be done was to measure the distance from the base to the corner of the "shebang" (B C), and subtract it from the altitude B T. The results obtained by these two methods were substantially the same.

A great deal of earth comes out of such a hole. It was estimated that we brought out two cart loads a day. For the first day or two our plan was simply to carry it from the cabin after dark. Now this might escape notice, but if it once attracted observation, and that observation should continue from night to night, detection was certain. The boldest course is always the safest, and therefore it was determined that all the earth should be carried out in broad daylight. Accordingly a number of officers were detailed for this work. They never went for a bucket of water without filling the bucket with earth; none carried out a bag or basket empty. Little by little, the contents of the tunnel were distributed around the camp. Some was thrown in the paths and trampled down—some in the ravine, and covered with ashes, and some was used to bank up "shebangs." It was scattered so perfectly that many of our own number were at a loss to know what had become of it.

A sentinel constantly watched the gate. When any Confederate visitor entered, a signal was given, the work stopped within the tunnel, and a blanket was spread over the shaft. Yet all these precautions did not satisfy our anxiety. The ingenious engineer of the "Diana" was again called in. He skilfully arched over the shaft, leaving a hole at one end, over which he placed the meal-box of the Hawk-eye. The bottom of this box was movable. When work was suspended in the tunnel the bag of meal and cooking utensils were thrown into the box, and it became as honest a looking box as a man could have. When work was to begin again the box was emptied, the bottom was lifted out, and there appeared a dark hole, through which a man could drop down into the shaft below.

Yet still our anxiety grew with the work. We knew that if suspicion ever fell on any "shebang" it would fall on this one. We, therefore, determined to push a sap to an inner cabin, and pass all the earth through to the less suspicious building. A wet morning gave us a pretext for digging a trench. The trench was speedily roofed and covered with earth. When fully completed, one end of it entered the shaft, and the other opened in the second "shebang." The operation then was this: a workman in the tunnel filled a small box with earth; a second one in the shaft drew out the box, and lifted it into the "baby-jumper" (as the sap was called); a third drew it through, and emptied it in the second "shebang."

Yet all this precaution was deemed insufficient. The "baby-jumper" was enlarged so that a man could crawl through; the box was removed, and the shaft was covered over entirely. On the very day that this was completed, the gate suddenly opened, and Colonel Allen came in. He walked rapidly to the Hawk-eye (whither he had never gone before), and contrary to his invariable custom, entered it unasked and unannounced. He saw only a bare earth floor.

It was plainly desirable that information of the projected movement should be sent to our army, and accordingly a message to that effect was duly forwarded to our lines by the Confederate authorities in the following letter:

CAMP FORD, *March* 19, 1864,

DEAR N——

"Letters came yesterday for some "of* us*, and it will please J—— to know that hers did "not *escape* this time. About a dozen of us have had "letters containing news to 15th ult. There were two from "mother, and one dated April 7th from C—— for me. "On the whole *we* will not complain of our luck. I "am even willing to scatter them more equally amongst the "prisoners, and indeed to let others have a few of mine.

"We feel certain the blockaders "at* Sabine* and Galveston keep ours. Maj. Hyllested "assures us, he sent a flag off with them at least "three times. Let F—— look out* for them. Some "were sent in September, others in October, November and "December, I think, but will not be sure as to all of "these months. Those which go *by Shreveport* and Red River "seem to get through and reach their destination in "*some* cases.

"Stevenson (as I wrote to you) whom "we left sick at Iberia, is here nearly well. Let "his family know this."

The key to this letter had been previously sent out by an exchanged prisoner. It early became apparent that secret correspondence might be useful to us and of advantage to the government. But it was necessary that it should be both secret and unsuspected. An ordinary cipher would have been as worthless as any contraband letter. My first idea was to take a certain word of every line to convey the hidden message. But this I found lengthened the letter too much, and I therefore added to these every blotted and underscored word. If a person were sure that his correspondent knew the key, and if he were allowed to coin facts and write nonsense, this correspondence would be easy enough. But it became somewhat difficult when written under the following conditions; viz., 1. To write briefly; 2. To use such words and subjects as a prisoner in that camp would naturally use; 3. To state in the body of the letter the personal information I wished to communicate; for I was never sure my key had reached my correspondent. Yet a very little practice removed much of the difficulty, and for six months, every letter carried out its twofold intelligence. If now the reader will collate the fifth word of every line, the words marked thus* and those in *italics*, the inner meaning of the foregoing letter will become apparent.

News now arrived of the advance of our army up the Red River. The leaves were coming out, and the time was slowly approaching when we expected to use the tunnel. The officer who had been selected to direct the work, well knew that when this time should arrive it would be absolutely impossible to prevent the whole camp from talking of it, and that one careless word might ruin everything. He therefore sought to conceal the real situation of the affair, by overrating the real distance to the tree, and underrating the amount of work actually performed. Every precaution was taken to divert attention from the progress of the work; for the inspection of the shrewd Colonel betokened that some foolish word had been overheard by the sentries, or else that we had a secret spy in camp. There were then a few straggling privates within the stockade, and suspicion pointed at two of these. A constant watch was kept upon them; and orders were given that all conversation on the subject should cease.

The night of the fifteenth of April would be the first on which the moon would rise late enough for a sufficient number of men to pass out; and on the fifteenth of April it was designed that the tunnel should be finished and the sally made. On the ninth, news arrived that a great battle had begun at Mansfield. On the tenth, rumors came, saying that the Confederate General had possessed sufficient courage to move forward and strike our invading army. On the eleventh, we heard that he had struck it in detail, routing it and driving it back toward Alexandria. On the thirteenth, Colonel Allen received orders to prepare for four thousand new prisoners. On the fifteenth, the stockade was moved back six hundred feet, and our unfortunate tunnel left high and dry in the middle of this new enclosure.

XI.

EXCHANGE.

The work upon the tunnel was interrupted for a day by an event, which I think must be without a parallel in any other prison-camp. At the breaking out of the rebellion, Miss Mollie Moore was a school girl of sixteen. After Galveston was re-taken by the Confederates, the "Houston Telegraph" was adorned with several heroic ballads, written by the young lady, whom the editor sometimes called "our pet," and sometimes the "unrivalled star of Texan literature." The 42d Massachusetts had been quartered in a warehouse on the wharf of Galveston, and had passed the night previous to their capture in fighting, all of which the ballad described thus:

> "Beneath the Texan groves the haughty foemen slept."

The literary taste of a simple, half-educated people is never very high, and it is not surprising that this childish composition so nicely equalled the taste of its readers, as to be deemed a marvel of genius, and actually to be published with General Magruder's official report. Miss Mollie became the literary genius of Texas, and her effusions were poured forth through the "Houston Telegraph" and the "Tyler Reporter" and the "Crocket

Quid Nunc" in most lavish streams. This strong incentive to write, and these ready opportunities to publish were not altogether abused by the young authoress, who rapidly improved. Judging her by the other poems that adorned those papers, she indeed appeared to be the "unrivalled star of Texan literature." I am fortunate in being able to introduce her toNorthern readers by an extract from:

AN INVITATION

TO MISS LIZZIE IRVINE, OF TYLER.

The autumn sunset's fairy dyes
Have faded from the bonding skies;
Grey twilight (she with down-cast eyes
And trailing garments) passeth by;
And thro' the cloud-rifts shine the stars,
As sunbeams burst thro' prison bars;
And on the soft wind, faintly heard,
The warbling of some twilight bird
Comes floating sylph-like, clad with power,
To whisper, "This is love's own hour!"

* * * * *

'Tis autumn—and with summer fell
The climbing vines of Sylvan Dell;
Our flowers too withered when the pall
Crept over summer; and the fall
Of dry leaves, eddying thro' the air,
Has left the tall trees brown and bare:
And more—at winter's high behest,
The crisp fern waves a tattered crest
Above the stream, whose crystal pride
The river-screen was wont to hide.

But think not all are faithless! no,
Not all doth Summer yield her foe,
Tho' Winter grasp each flower and vine—
He cannot claim the fadeless pine;
And high upon our rough hill-steeps,
His watch the crested holly keeps.
Ah would that Love could thus defy
The storms that sweep our wintry sky!

* * * * *

Come wander with me where the hill
Slopes downward to the waters still,
Where bright among the curling vines
The sevres berry scarlet shines.
And on yon brown hill's bosky side,
Where flames the sumach's crimson pride,
The steeps and tangled thickets glow
With rude persimmons golden show;
And down the dell, where daylight's beams
Make golden pathways by the streams,
Where whispering winds are never mute,
The hawthorn hangs her ebon fruit.

It seems impossible that a young lady able to write such pleasing verse, could descend to this:

Let our flag kiss the breeze! let it float o'er the field!
Not a heart will grow faint, not a bay'net will yield.

Chorus—It shall never be lowered, the black flag we bear,
It shall never, never, never, no never, etc., etc., etc.

Yet before our departure, the young authoress, abandoning her barbarous teachings, rose in style and sentiment from "The Black Flag" (as she called her inflated nonsense) to a little poem, of which the following stanzas are, perhaps, imperfectly repeated:

Morn dawned upon the contest—the bugle blast
Wound out its shrilly summons, and the word
Leaped down the lines, and fiery hearts beat fast;
Two gallant armies bared the glittering sword,
And fearless breasted battle's bitter waves,
And eager thousands sought their nameless graves
By the river of death.

* * * * *

A single thought swept o'er him, and his eye
Grew troubled for one moment—then 'twas o'er.
His fair young wife—his dark-eyed babe, to die
Far from them! The cannon's lordly roar
Broke on his ear—his eye caught back its pride—
His lax hand grasped the glittering sword—he died
By the river of death.

He died, and night with clouded skies looked down
Upon his burial! The torch-light red
Glared fitfully about; they gathered round—
His comrades, sadly silent, near the dead.
They wrapped him in his blanket—song and prayer
Awoke the stillness as they laid him there,
By the river of death.

"Buried upon the field!" 'Tis meet; for why
Should warriors rest where peaceful churchyards are?
Why should they sleep where battle's trumpet cry
Was never heard? nor breath of glorious war?
No! on *their* field of glory—on the plain
Where Death's grand chorus hushed the noble slain—
There let them lie!

There was a young lieutenant among the prisoners given to collecting all sorts of scraps and curiosities, and so he addressed a note to Miss Mollie, begging for her autograph and copies of any poems she might be able to spare. Within a reasonable time there came a copy of the "Invitation" and an autograph of the "Black Flag," and a reproachful letter to Lieutenant Pearson. There was also a letter to Colonel Allen, not intended for Yankee reading. It expressed a little repentance for writing so cruelly to an unfortunate prisoner—avowed a wish to treat even invaders with politeness, and wound up with the Eve-like conclusion, "But I could not resist the temptation. Yours truly, Mollie E. Moore."

One or two other causes at the same time combined to induce Miss Mollie to visit Camp Ford, and one lucky morning Mrs. Allen escorted her in. She was one of those girls that men are a little afraid of, and that other girls do not like. She had a slender figure, a thin face, light hair, light blue, dreamy eyes, and she was accompanied by the object of the "Invitation." There was not much of the poetess in her bearing—practical, very neatly dressed, a ready talker, and quite sharp at repartee. Yet when Colonel Burrill was presented to her as one of the "haughty foemen," she colored, and showed a little pretty embarrassment. The friend was her exact opposite, with dark hair, dark eyes, very shy and silent and reserved, and much the prettiest Texan it was ever my luck to see.

About the same time a second notable incident occurred, being no less than a literary contest between prisoners and the outside world. One of our number had received some attention from the Houston editor, in return for which he sent him a few verses, entitled, "Pax Vobiscum." These lines so exactly accorded with the yearning for peace, that they awakened great interest, and after a while were re-published, with the editorial avowal that they were written by a Yankee prisoner. Another literary lady, middle-aged, married, and rather stout (so I was informed), but who called herself by the infantile name of "Maggie of Marshall," thereupon came out with a poem, addressed to "the noble prisoner," in which she styled him, "The northern by birth but the southern in soul," and urged him to come straight over and fight on their side. The "noble prisoner" had no earthly intention of deserting, so he wrote a second poem for the "Tyler Reporter," in which he defined his position. When Mistress Maggie of Marshall found that her blandishments were all thrown away, she became deeply indignant, and immediately wrote her second poem for the "Reporter," wherein the "noble prisoner" was turned into a puritan and a murderer and a son of Cain, and finally turned adrift with the contemptuous pity:

> "Behold this Ephraim to his idols joined—
> Let him alone."

I cannot speak very explicitly of our last three months. In telling this story, I have tried to picture only the better side of everything, and to make it imprisonment with the unpleasant parts left out. The story is "the truth," but not "the whole truth," and does not deny or conflict with the narratives of others. A sense of honor forbids that the better actions of our late enemies should be hidden, or that the good and the bad should be condemned together. Yet I may as well add here, for the benefit of certain persons, that the respect yielded to a Southern Soldier standing by his State, and heroically fighting for that false belief in which he was bred, does not extend to those cowards who, "*sympathizing* with the South," have skulked through the war behind the generous protection of the United States.

The Red River prisoners arrived, and were followed by numbers from Arkansas. Our soldiers and sailors of Camp Groce, who, four months before, left us hopefully sure of their release, came back—I need not say how sad and disappointed. Our number swelled from a hundred officers, to forty-seven hundred and twenty-five, officers, soldiers and sailors. Then followed a quarter of a year of loathsome wretchedness, beside which, the squallor and vice of a great city's worst haunts appeared—and still appear, too bright and pure to yield a comparison.

The healthy character of our camp changed in a single week. Disease and death followed each other quickly in. The friendless sick lay shelterless on the ground around us, the sun scorching and blighting them by day, and the cold Texan night-wind smiting them by night. We walked over the dying and the dead, whenever we moved, and saw and heard their miseries through every hour. Beside the gate stood a pile of coffins, reminding all who went out and came in, of their probable impending fate. The vice and lawlessness that live in the vile haunts of cities sprang up and flourished here. The Confederate troops (idle after their victories on the Red River) came back to scour the country for deserters; and our unhappy conscript friends whispered that escape was hopeless now, and sought to comfort us by lamenting that no dim prospect of exchange cheered them. Our kind friends, the Allens, had gone, and the English Lieutenant-Colonel, who commanded, treated a few with surly civility, but the great mass with brutal cruelty. The horrors of these great prison-camps are not yet told—will never be.

It is darkest before the dawn. We sat at dinner, one day, and a sailor, whose nick-name was Wax, came to the door, and said to his Captain, "The paroling officer, sir, who was here three months ago, has come back, and the guards say, there are some of us to be exchanged." The Captain thanked the man, and we went on with our dinner. "I suppose," some one remarked, "that if exchange ever does come, the news will come through Wax;" and then we dropped the subject; for a hundred times just such stories had been told, and a hundred times they had proved false. Captain Dillingham finished his dinner, and said he would go out and see that officer; perhaps the fellow had brought us some letters. The Captain came back in a few minutes, and said, as cheerily as though he were telling good news for himself, "You are to go, and I am to stay—none of us navy fellows to be exchanged." Our rose had its thorn.

Three days of anxious waiting passed, and we bade our naval friends farewell. Some of them had been tried then six months longer than we had been. The trial of all went on for seven months more. They suffered, again and again, the sorest pain that can be inflicted on prisoners of war—the sight of those marching out who were captured long subsequent to themselves, and the fear that the injustice comes from the neglect of their own government. There was thrown upon them also a strong temptation; for there were desertions, I am sorry to say, from the army. The deserters were chiefly foreign born, but not all. The first, indeed, was a young man in the 2d Rhode Island Cavalry, a native of another New England State. Yet these sailors never faltered. If men who have fought bravely in battle, and who have been faithful through suffering, ever deserved to be welcomed home with honors and ovations, then did these sailors of the "Morning Light," "Clifton," and "Sachem."

One thousand of us marched out of the crowded camp, We inhaled long breaths of the pure untainted air, yet dared not believe that this would end in exchange. It was the sixth time that some had passed over the same road, and we might well be incredulous. There was weary marching over burning sand, and the long-con fined men grew weak and foot-sore, before they had marched an hour. The Confederate officers acted kindly, but the prisoners had seen chances of exchange lost by a single day's delay, and they dragged themselves forward with a rigor that would have been cruelty had it been enforced on them. The white sand glaring under their feet, and the burning sun beating down through the breathless air, made a fiery ordeal. Shoeless men, with feet seared and blistered so that the hot sand felt like coals of fire, tottered along, not faster than a mile an hour, yet moving steadily. A few wagons, pressed from the harvest-fields, were covered with the sick and dying, and thus appearing, on the fifth day, we marched through the streets of Shreveport.

Here three days of insupportable longness awaited us; for Shreveport had been the dam that had always stopped prisoners and turned them back. On the fourth morning we marched on board of the steamboats that were to carry us down the Red River; and then, when Shreveport was fairly behind us, we breathed freer, and for the first time allowed ourselves to hope. At Alexandria we were stopped and landed, and made to endure two other days of suspense, but at last we re-embarked for the point of exchange.

The mouth of Red River was the place where our flag-of-truce boat was to meet us. We reached it before sunrise, and saw again the muddy current of the Mississippi. No flag-of-truce boat was in sight. But we saw two gun-boats that sentinelled the river, and our eyes rested on the flag that streamed over their decks, and silently proclaimed to us the still sovereign power of the United States. A shot from the gun-boats bade us stop. A small boat was lowered; we saw its crew enter it, and an officer come over the side; and then it pulled toward us. The officer inquired the object of the Confederate flag-of-truce, and told us the disheartening fact that he had heard nothing of this exchange. Then followed nine hours, that seemed as though they would never move away. A crowd of prisoners stood on the upper deck, their eyes strained on the river. The morning passed, the afternoon began, and still nothing could be seen. At two o'clock, a little puff of black smoke appeared far down the Mississippi, and a murmur ran through the crowd. An hour crawled away, and a large, white steamer pushed around a headland of the river, and came rapidly up against the muddy current. The strained eyes thought they saw a white flag, but it was hard to distinguish it on the white back-ground of the boat. Suddenly the steamer turned and ran in to the bank below us—the white flag streamed out plainly in view, and the decks were covered with Confederate prisoners.

It was on the last day of thirteen months of captivity that I re-entered our lines. All that I had seen and learnt was contained in about thirty days. Could these thirty days have been brought together, they would have formed an interesting and instructive month. But beside this one were twelve other months, that were a dreary, idle waste. They formed a year that had brought no pleasure, profit or instruction. Some who entered it young, came out with broken health and shortened lives; some who entered it in middle age, came out with grey hair, impaired memory, and the decrepitude of premature old age. It was a year that had taken much from us and given to us little in return. A year of ever-disappointed hopes, of barren promises, of a blank and dreary retrospect. Contemplating it, we might almost reverse the meaning of our gently-chiding poet:

"Rich gift of God! A year of time!
What pomp of rise and shut of day—
What hues wherewith our northern clime
Makes autumn's drooping woodlands gay—
What airs outblown from ferny dells,
And clover bloom, and sweet-brier smells—
What songs of brooks and birds—what fruits and flowers,
Green woods and moon-lit snows have in its round been ours."

www.ingramcontent.com/pod-product-compliance
Lightning Source LLC
LaVergne TN
LVHW011215110826
845150LV00006B/1434

* 9 7 8 1 4 2 5 5 1 6 7 5 8 *